BEYOND
THE
WINDOWSILL

Add Style to Your Home with the Beauty of Indoor Plants

Special Note to Seasoned Gardeners

Regarding Latin names and common names: Latin names for plants are the same everywhere (although they may change over time). Common names, on the other hand, vary all over the world, even across town. Therefore, why did I prefer the use of common names when introducing plants in this book?

During my career, I have found that Latin names often alienate and intimidate beginning gardeners. Common names are often indicative of a plant's origin, appearance, and behavior, and have a charm that is comforting to me and to many other gardeners. The purpose of this book is to revitalize America's passion for interior plants. Therefore, I have relaxed a few formalities in an effort to improve our success. I respectfully request that seasoned gardeners accommodate this approach so as to encourage more introductions to nature and the wonderful world of interior plants.

–Jon Carloftis

Published by Cool Springs Press
101 Forrest Crossing Boulevard, Suite 100
Franklin, Tennessee 37064

Catalog in Publication Data is Available.
ISBN: 1591862639

First printing 2006
Printed in the United States of America

10 9 8 7 6 5 4 3 2 1

Photography by Helen Norman

Jon Carloftis is available for speaking engagements.
Visit www.mckinneyspeakers.com or call 800-955-4746 for information.

Visit the author's website at www.JonCarloftis.com

Managing Editor: Ramona D. Wilkes
Cover and Interior Design: Emily Keafer for Anderson Thomas Design
Copyediting: Sally Graham
Horticulture Editing: Teri Rice

Visit the Cool Springs Press website at www.coolspringspress.net

BEYOND THE WINDOWSILL

Add Style to Your Home with the Beauty of Indoor Plants

JON CARLOFTIS

COOL SPRINGS PRESS

This book is dedicated to all of the gardeners who are making this world a more beautiful place for everyone.

ACKNOWLEDGEMENTS

"In this world, anything is possible."

To my parents, thank you for this sentiment. Given your endless encouragement, I have discovered that with hard work, perseverance and an open mind, everything is, in fact, possible. Thank you.

Helen Norman, thank you again for taking amazing photographs – you are the best. Dan Stack, for assisting Helen and always putting us in the right light. Dale Fisher, for endless editing and daily encouragement. Elaine Fisher, for ongoing research and text. To my professors at the University of Kentucky, Sharon Bale and Bob Anderson, who introduced me and countless others to a whole new world – that of interior plants. Pat at Parker's Nursery and Jeff and Kathy at Geerling's Nursery for introducing me to new plant varieties and making work such a pleasure. Parkside Orchids, for their vast selection of orchids – inside your greenhouses, I am always on vacation.

To my clients: Darrel Flanel, Lisa and Steve Hankin, and Lauren Howard, for allowing me to photograph in your beautiful homes. My wonderful crew in New York: Jorge Androver, Carlos Rodriguez, Lance Roussarie and Mattias Stebbins, for excellent work. And Cindy Games and Ramona Wilkes of Cool Springs Press, for having faith in my vision.

Thank you all. Collectively we will make the world a little greener, and a little more beautiful.

–Jon Carloftis

"The real voyage of discovery consists of not only seeking new landscapes, but in having new eyes."

MARCEL PROUST

TABLE OF CONTENTS ○

INTRODUCTION: GARDENING IS MY LIFE

From the cold days in winter dreaming of the rich, earthy smells of spring soon to come, to the last golden dry days of fall, **I AM CONSUMED** with thoughts of plants and gardening.

When discussing this passion with others, as well as my passion for pets and antique cars, I'm sometimes looked at with puzzlement and disbelief. How can someone be so passionate about anything, particularly plants?

But I am a firm believer that if they, as a child, were given the chance to...

> plant a seed,
> water it,
> nurture it, and
> watch it grow...

they would have stood a good chance of being hooked. With ongoing study and real life experience they may have developed their own unique passion for plants and perhaps a better understanding of others who are as passionate as I am.

My introduction to plants began well before my official school years, on a wooded path cleared along Kentucky's Rockcastle River. Along this two-mile path, Daddy and I took weekly journeys to bleed a single water supply line running from a fresh-water spring upstream to our home built on the bank of the river. Daddy sparked my passion for plants by challenging me to learn the names of every living thing along the way.

In second grade, a simple science class experiment – the planting of grass seed in a pickle jar – made me more aware of the importance of healthy soil, sunlight, and proper watering. College horticulture classes allowed me access to previously unknown flora and fauna growing inside University of Kentucky greenhouses.

It's during the past twenty years of real-life experience creating gardens atop New York rooftops that my passion for plants and gardening has grown strongest. Client demands were for the seemingly impossible: beautiful plants that worked in the harshest conditions, healthy gardens that thrived from year to year, and results that complimented their unique sense of style. **I AM CONSUMED.**

Beyond the Windowsill was written to offer a unique look at the way indoor plants can transform even the nicest house into a home. You will be surprised at how a plant breathes life into a room – giving it color, interest, balance, and warmth.

I wrote this book to inspire all kinds of people. The person who thinks interior plants are old fashioned, out-of-style, and retired, or naysayers who may recall a clutter of neglected plants merely lined up along available windowsills and next to glass doors. This book will likely change their perception of interior plants forever. *Beyond the Windowsill* is for the non-plant-enthusiasts who, despite their disposition, realize a beautiful orchid can change a whole room. And it's for practical beginners who want an introduction to indoor plants and instructions to ensure first-time success. Even experienced horticulturalists and gardeners who are already passionate about plant life will find some ideas to liven-up their home.

Martha Stewart rekindled America's passion for entertaining outdoors, a passion lost in the '60s and '70s given America's newly developed interest in the benefits of everything "instant" and "time-saving." With this book I want to revitalize America's passion for the beauty of the *indoors* – made even better with the addition of indoor plants.

LIFE IN THE ROOM

Every room in your home calls for a bit of life.

Some of my fondest memories are of rolling back the rug in the living room to dance to big band music with family and friends after a holiday dinner and witnessing the blowing out of candles on a birthday cake. On a quieter note, I've always loved reading a book in front of the fireplace in the company of my healthy, yellow Labradors. My dog Bertha was sure to lay her head in my lap while her mother, Daisy – named after my favorite flower – would be fast asleep at my feet.

Not everyone can enjoy these pleasures. A small apartment, a dorm room, retirement home living, or a demanding job often prevents the joys of family gatherings or owning a pet. But I contend everyone still has the place, the time, and the longing for a living thing in their home.

The "right" plant can introduce life to any room, instantly improving the look and feel of a home. Plants do this in many ways. Some become the focal point of a room. Others enhance what's already there, blending seamlessly with the décor. Some shout "look at me" with their attractive shape and color. Some merely whisper their greeting and quietly offer comfort as you go about your business.

The Purpose of Plants

- **MAKE CONNECTIONS:** A plant placed in just the right location can seamlessly connect the inside of a home with the outside, as if there were no wall at all. The right container can help with this as well. A well-planned container can connect different plants within a room for a more unified look, or continue a decorative theme already defined by furniture or accessories.

- **ADD PRIVACY:** Placed properly, a plant can create privacy in a way that is still welcoming and attractive. While obscuring a window view, a plant allows sunlight to enter, offering an alternative to window coverings.

- **CREATE A MOOD:** With its shape or foliage, a plant can introduce a bit of needed drama or softness to a room, changing the mood. Its mere presence in a space can encourage a more relaxed and pensive feeling or add needed energy. Plant choices for low-light are available to further enhance an already softly-lit room.

- **SHOWCASE AN ATTRACTIVE VIEW:** Framing a photo or painting places emphasis on the subject. Likewise, with a beautiful view, framing each side with plantings guides the eye in the desired direction.

- **BLOCK AN UNATTRACTIVE VIEW:** Most people have them somewhere in their home, and a well-chosen plant will take attention away from the background. We use plants outside to hide air-conditioners, trashcans, and neighbors – why not use them inside as well?

- **CREATE BALANCE:** The size and shape of plants can be utilized to create balance in a room – symmetrically or asymmetrically, it's a matter of taste. Use plants to offset small or large accessories as needed.

- **PROTECT INTERIORS:** Although not as protective as a closed shade, a dense leaf covering will help prevent sun damage to fabrics, floor coverings and important keepsakes.

As you'll see in this chapter, a single plant can offer many benefits to a home. They are eager to please.

Symmetry in a room is pleasing to most people and adds a formal feeling to a room. Twin *corn plants* underplanted with *English ivy* (above) are centered over the couch's end pillows along the windowsill in my family room, while more English ivy topped with a touch of *African violets* (below) is centered in front of the middle pillow to maintain the desired balance.

PLANT PURPOSE: CREATE BALANCE

Bonsai plants add drama with an air of sophistication and old world charm. However, they require steady attention, which may be a bit problematic for the busy traveler or forgetful person. **PLANT PURPOSE: CREATE A SOPHISTICATED MOOD**

Libraries are often dark and dreary places. Low-light tolerant *rhapis palm* underplanted with *fittonia* adds liveliness to an otherwise austere room. **Plant Purpose: Lighten a Mood**

Even the smallest of bathrooms have special spots for a soothing, green plant. Bathroom plants are the easiest to maintain given they have ready sources of moisture and water. A souvenir silver mint julep cup from the Kentucky Derby makes a sophisticated home for *English ivy* (sink), while a five-and-dime clay pot does the trick for a *rabbit's foot fern* (floor). **Plant Purpose: Create a Soothing Mood**

This gentle *peace lily* in its wicker basket and a cool breeze from a small fan are sure to promote a relaxed feeling. The view of the road 15 feet from the house disappears given the size and placement of this plant. **PLANT PURPOSES: BLOCK AN UNATTRACTIVE VIEW; CREATE A CALMING MOOD**

This unique 1920s plant stand with arched supports has plenty of room for additional plants, but that option is declined to keep proper focus on the simple *golden pothos*. Potted in a beautiful white ceramic container and placed on the top shelf – it creates a bit more privacy in the window. The *arrowhead plant* rests comfortably below. Remember to move floor plants away from any heating systems before the cooler fall and winter months arrive.

PLANT PURPOSE:
ADD PRIVACY

This old workbench by my dining room window is the perfect spot to showcase these beautiful *succulents*, while providing my dining room with a bit of needed privacy from neighbors during their after-dinner strolls. Everyone gets a chance to admire them from my front porch swing, outside my front dining room window, or while entering the side entrance of my farmhouse. The addition of pumpkins in the fall and moss- and lichen-covered sticks in the spring will keep this arrangement fresh from season to season.

Plant Purpose:

Add Privacy

Think outside the box when deciding on the perfect container for your plants. A playful cement birdbath gets reassigned as a planter for *English ivy* and *Cuban oregano* on my back porch, to help bring the outside in.
PLANT PURPOSE: MAKE A CONNECTION

The long shelf and windowsill above this bathtub provides plenty of room for this collection of white McCoy pottery filled with serene ferns. The *holly fern* (left) and the *Boston fern* pair (right) are light enough to join the *asparagus fern* (center) on the windowsill should a bit more privacy be needed. **PLANT PURPOSE: ADD PRIVACY**

This otherwise dark and cool corner table is brightened with a mirror, twin lucite lamps with beaded shades, and a *dwarf schefflera*. Unlike larger *scheffleras*, the dwarf variety grows happily in low-light conditions.

PLANT PURPOSE:
LIGHTEN A MOOD

Narrow hallways have little-to-no room for larger plants. Because of the limited "parking space," place smaller, compact plants such as *fittonia* in smaller pots along the windowsill. These serve as a nice reminder to steal a glance of the outdoors.
PLANT PURPOSE: MAKE CONNECTIONS

What better way to invite the out-doors in, than this ceiling-to-floor screened-in porch surrounded by beautiful gardens? A stone planter with *baby's tears* adds color and life to this room and helps to connect these two worlds. **PLANT PURPOSE: MAKE A CONNECTION**

Not every plant has to be a wallflower. The *English ivy* (top left), *heart-leaf philodendron* (left bottom), *grape ivy* (windowsill left), and *kalanchoe* (windowsill right) fill the wall while the *lime light dracaena* trio takes center stage on the floor of this room of chocolate brown furnishings and neutral flooring. The dracaenas demonstrate that plants can be used to camouflage a bit of clutter. A *spider plant* (peeking in from lower bottom right) adds interest to a bare space under a garden plant stand.

PLANT PURPOSE: BLOCK AN UN-ATTRACTIVE VIEW

Larger plants such
as this sun-loving
schefflera can be used
like screens to protect
interior furniture and
prevent sensitive
fabrics from fading.
PLANT PURPOSE:
PROTECT INTERIOR

A great dining room is often the jewel of the home. Here matching *Buddhist pines* frame the amazing view of a church steeple while softening the edges of the oversized patio doors. **PLANT PURPOSE: SHOWCASE AN ATTRACTIVE VIEW**

An unused doorway need not stick out like a sore thumb. This *Chinese fan palm* displayed atop a small oriental stool provides the perfect cover, and a beautiful one too. **PLANT PURPOSE: BLOCK AN UNATTRACTIVE VIEW**

BEFORE & AFTER

What a difference a day makes. . . especially if spent at the local nursery. Look what a few of my favorite interior plants have done to beautify these rooms.

BEFORE: Many beautiful homes are decorated with simplicity. Room clutter and changes in wall color are sacrificed in order to showcase the room and furniture designs, and select objects of art. This room with its earth-tone walls, cherry furniture with clean lines, a straight staircase, minimal adornments, and stark, white painted floors is appealing to me. But what's missing is any sign of life. Is anyone home?

AFTER: A *spider plant* with equally interesting shape and spiky foliage becomes a welcome and living object of art. To help it retain its shape, shoots can be cut from this plant, rooted in water, and then planted to start new plants.

AFTER: Plants were placed on the floor in the room above to avoid blocking important light and warmth. The handsome *Swiss cheese plant* (right) with large, triangular, translucent leaves introduces bright new color and contrasting shape without adding additional bulk. The *zz plant* (far left) – a kid's favorite with thick, dark-green spear-shaped leaves reminiscent of dinosaur tails – is the perfect draw for young readers. A pair of *succulents* (table) appears to glow on center stage.

BEFORE: Contrasting color, shape, and softness are missing in this small and rugged but austere reading room decorated in muted colors and dominant rectangular shapes.

BEFORE: This expansive space characteristic of downtown city lofts (with two-story, single-color walls and ceilings; and large windows and doors) can prove challenging when you're attempting to add warmth to the entertainment area. An open staircase often draw guests' attention away from the party.

AFTER: Keeping with the room's proportions, large interior plants were added to oversized furniture and artwork to establish balance in the room. This tall and voluminous *parlor palm* with *English ivy* underplanting (lower right) not only adds a bit of privacy but also provides the structure, color, and interest in the foreground to counter the openness of the loft and the large, colorful painting (upper left). The *dwarf schefflera* (lower left) and *cast iron plant* (upper left) soften a previously empty corner and help define a smaller, cozier space more inviting to guests downstairs.

SIX STEPS TO A BEAUTIFUL ROOM

The right plant can differ from room to room.

I believe that every room in a home can benefit from a breath of fresh air with the addition of the right plant. Given that no two rooms are exactly alike in structure, physical characteristics, intended use, or décor – the "right" plant often differs from room to room. Would you expect a single gift to please everyone in your family during the holidays? Of course not; each expresses different tastes and expectations. It's the same with a room. But how does one go about picking the right plant? Following is my step-by-step approach to introducing the right interior plant into any room.

STEP 1: *Establish the Plant's Purpose and Placement*

What do you want to accomplish in your home with indoor plants? As I've said, plants introduce life and warmth into every room. I consider this to be a plant's **PRIMARY PURPOSE**. Simply introducing any plant into any room is guaranteed to spark a smile and friendly conversation (*What kind of plant is it? Where did it come from? Who is it for?*). That alone is worth the sticker price.

However, before choosing your plant, it is best to establish its **SECONDARY PURPOSE** and **LIKELY PLACEMENT**. I covered plant purposes in more detail in chapter 1:

- Make connections
- Add privacy
- Create a mood
- Showcase an attractive view
- Block an unattractive view
- Create balance
- Protect interiors

STEP 2: *Determine the Correct Light Conditions*

Part of the fun of using plants is finding the right spot. Many people believe that interior plants can survive only on windowsills or if placed near French glass doors. This is a misconception that can lead to a cluttered room, room inbalance, and sometimes your plants' untimely death. You need to know that every plant can be described as either a low-light, medium-light, or high-light lover.

It has taken me awhile to figure out just where some of my plants such as my **JADE** and **SCHEFFLERA** are happiest in my home. When you have found the best light conditions for your interior plant, it will let you know with fresh new leaves. In contrast, plant growth and posture will be sacrificed when it is unhappy. Plants aren't too different from people. Plants just let you know how they are feeling much more subtly.

I could bore you with textbook answers of how a plant needs light according to specs such as "watts per square meter" – thank goodness for the nice people who figure this stuff out. But all people usually want to know are the basics. Most people consider plants in the same way they do cars. They need only the basics about car maintenance to ensure their cars get them where they are going. Most of us remain far less interested in understanding the physics of internal combustion.

Because my 150-year-old farmhouse is one room deep, the addition of windows and doors makes it feel as if I'm living in a treehouse – surrounded by beautiful green foliage. It also allows me to enjoy plants that require high-light conditions.

To keep things simple, I've provided this chapter with a few general guidelines regarding plant placement. As you'll see, many plants will thrive well beyond the windowsill.

Using South, West, or East Windows

With a measuring tape, measure the area from a windowsill to 5 feet away from the uncovered window. This area should be reserved for high-light plants. The area 5 to 10 feet away from the uncovered window is good for medium-light plants. The area beyond (10 to 15 feet away from the uncovered window) is best for low-light plants.

It's important to know that morning light through an east window is less intense than evening light through a west window, or light anytime through a south window. Therefore, medium- and low-light plants in an east window may be moved a bit closer to the light than in south or west windows.

This pair of medium-light *arrowhead vine* is suited for this windowsill because of its northern and tree-shaded exposure. The dense foliage from top to bottom provides this room with a bit more privacy, perfect for a window without shade or curtain.

Note that most plants will slowly die if placed beyond 15 feet from a south, west, or east window.

Using North Windows

The area from the windowsill to 5 feet away from the uncovered window is suitable for high- to medium-light plants. The area beyond (5 to 10 feet away from the uncovered window) is good for low-light plants.

The majority of plants will slowly die if placed beyond 10 feet from a north window.

In general, the majority of lower-light plants can readily adapt to higher-light conditions; therefore you can cheat by placing low- or medium-light plants 1 to 2 inches closer to a light source than generally stated. This will not harm the plant. On the other hand, higher-light plants are more sensitive and will suffer if exposed to lower-light conditions.

Keep in mind that even a sheer curtain or the partial shade of an outdoor tree can change the dynamics of these guidelines. Begin by following these general guidelines, but keep a close watch on a new interior plant to determine if it needs to be relocated.

STEP 3: *Grow Comfortable with Larger Plants*

Once the ideal location has been chosen, the confines of the surrounding space will often dictate the size of the plant you can use. Keep in mind that the plant doesn't need to fill *all* the available space, simply enough of the space to accomplish your mission. If a plant you want is slightly too big, a simple pruning may help. Some larger plants may be necessary depending on the what you want to accomplish. Don't be nervous – it just takes a little planning.

Some people can mentally complete a room with absolutely nothing in it. Others need to see it completed before determining whether it will work for them. Although often necessary, the latter approach is time-consuming and sometimes frustrating. Therefore, I've developed a way to "see" my plan for a room without investing in the plant.

To do this, I introduce an artificial shape of similar size. I will stuff a garbage bag with newspaper, for example, and place it in the designated spot to get a sense of how the plant will relate to the existing space and what size will work best.

The tall and slender high-light *golden variegated schefflera* is picture perfect. It adds warmth to this room without blocking the view of the beautiful gardens outdoors. The colors of this plant complement both indoor and outdoor color palettes to make for a seamless transition of both worlds. An old wooden plant container fits the decor of the room.

There is nothing pleasing to see from this kitchen window looking directly onto the plain brick building next door. But don't cover a view like this with a shade and block needed sunlight. Instead, allow your window box to frame an alternative focal point, like the high-light *Ming aralia*. The white porcelain container is perfectly in keeping with this room's contemporary flair.

STEP 4: *Choose the Right Plant for Your Style*

Once you have established the correct light category from which your plant can be selected (low, medium, or high as determined in **STEP 2**), take things a step further by selecting the right plant based on your sense of style. Consider the furniture in the room and the theme you've already established. Is there a plant that will continue that theme? For example, an indoor bamboo is a natural choice for a room with a tropical theme.

Now, before you grab your list and dash to the store for the perfect plant that will complement your décor and enhance your quality of life, reconsider **STEP 1**. Make sure the plant you have your eye on will accomplish what you hoped for in the first place!

STEP 5: *Accessorize with Out-of-the-Box Containers*

Every plant requires some type of container. A stylish choice does not have to be expensive. If you're creative, the most common things can be used in uncommon ways to produce the perfect solution. For example, find a container never intended for a plant. Consider a barrel, an old wooden toolbox, a ceramic bowl, or a silver ice bucket. (Don't forget a waterproof tray to prevent water damage, or a deeper cachepot with stones at the bottom to prevent the roots from sitting in water.) Your container options are limited only by your imagination.

STEP 6: *Commit to the Relationship*

This isn't your grandmother's *African violet* (medium light). Actually it is, but after a needed makeover. How different this old-fashioned plant looks in a modern silver-colored bowl on organic wood counters. Old looks new again!

You've given a lot of thought to your plant choices and to making them feel at home. Now you need to practice proper plant care to maintain the beauty of your new room. Remember – care must be consistent, but it's no more difficult than vacuuming a rug or dusting a table. I'll cover what you need to know in chapter 8.

The polka-dotted leaves of this high-light *hypoestes* nestled in a baby-blue wooden pot is perfectly in keeping with the theme and color of the treasured painting showcased in the background.

The happiest plants grow in rich soil. This healthy low-light *mother-in-law's tongue* makes that statement in this abstract display of retired greenhouse signage and packing crates. The rusted bucket used is a perfect match for the rusted steel letters.

This antique theater "accessory" in the center of this photo sheds light on the new additions to this room. Fresh curly willow branches flank the graceful, yet dramatic leaves of a medium-light *bird's nest fern* (background). The *wheatgrass* center-piece on the coffee table is a welcome sight to a nature lover in the dead of winter. If planted outdoors, curly willow branches will develop root systems and grow leaves, ultimately maturing into trees.

Use plants to define your space and to make it cozier. *Dracaena* plants with sword-shaped leaves would make a houseguest who's afraid of heights feel much more comfortable along this balcony. Limbs of the medium-light *night-blooming cereus* (right) dangle in the sunlight to produce beautiful plant profiles on the floor.

Block the bad view from this potting shed, or provide privacy using an oversized plant with a strong profile. The adaptable and masculine *zz **plant*** can go from full sun to deep shade.

The adaptive nature of the medium-light *arrowhead vine* makes it appropriate for a medium-light area (left of table) or a northern windowsill (right). Color is introduced in this monochromatic room without adding more furniture or artwork to the already cozy space. The plants selected have bright, lime green leaves and are short enough not to interfere with any parlor room conversations.

For mirrored tables, pick plants with foliage that is as attractive underneath as it is on top. Not everyone's backside is as pretty as that belonging to the high-light *blushing philodendron.*

This antique mirror and medium-light *moth orchid* are perfectly matched. While the orchid's branches are fine enough that one can still see a reflection, the antique mirror provides the orchid lover with double the blooms. Try mixing different plants on the same table. The pair of white high-light *kalanchoe* is set back to showcase the beautiful French vase and orchid in front.

When decorating inside or outside in the garden, balance and proportion are the foundations to creating the perfect setting. Though asymmetrically arranged, these medium-light *bird's nest ferns* are combined with a few family treasures to create a balance of shapes and textures. A peaceful vignette between two bedrooms is the outcome.

MY FAVORITE
INTERIOR PLANTS

The number of great plants could make your head spin.

Which plants are best suited to your home? Given their need for seasonal change, many plants to which we are accustomed outdoors – boxwoods (my favorite), apple trees, and roses – would never be suited for the indoors. And unless you live in a greenhouse, there isn't enough light, humidity, or constant temperature for anything but the toughest tropicals and a few select desert plant varieties. But despite these constraints, literally thousands upon thousands of plants remain from which to choose.

With this chapter I offer some selections to get you started. To make this list more manageable, I have built this chapter on sixty of my favorite interior plants – twenty plants within each of the three main light categories of low-, medium-, and high-light. The plants identified are by no means the *only* ones I would use or expect you to consider. It's merely a beginning.

Some plants are not included as "favorites" here because of their reputation for being a bit temperamental. (An example of this would be the **MING ARALIA** seen on page 39.) Once you've gained experience caring for the easier, less temperamental plants, you can undertake the care of the more temperamental ones.

My success with more difficult plants did not take place without a bit of help from old friends. College textbooks were dusted off so that I could reacquaint myself with familiar plant "faces." To learn more about the newer varieties now available through advancements in plant science, I consulted plant specialists at local nurseries. From this collective wisdom, I developed criteria to compare leading candidates fairly. Use the same criteria to select your "best in show."

Appearance:

Is the plant attractive to you? Given that beauty is in the eye of the beholder, it's important that **YOU** answer the question since the plant is coming home with **YOU**. You are likely to find it attractive if it's rich in colors that you enjoy (Notice the paint colors you've used in your home or the color of clothes you wear). Its profile and the shape and texture of its foliage should also appeal to your sense of style.

Are you a lover of modern decors? Most pointed, upright plants with their unique and firm textured foliage are attractive to the lover of modern decors. On the other hand, interior plants that resemble outdoor favorites are commonly the first choice of lovers of traditional homes.

Remember that no plant is attractive if it is unhealthy. Inspect your plant carefully for any indication of plant disease (see chapter 8) before heading for the checkout counter.

Care:

Given our busy lives spent caring for families, friends, and pets, as well as the time spent managing demanding careers, little time is available for much of anything. Therefore any plants requiring a lot of coddling did not make my "A" list. Weekly watering, seasonal feeding, and perhaps the occasional repotting are to be expected. Before buying a plant, refer to the "special" plant care instructions on the plant profile pages in this chapter to determine if the extra responsibility will put you over the edge. For the beginner, I recommend you get your feet wet with a single plant to determine your true propensity for nurturing our green friends.

Are you commonly away from home for two or three weeks at a time on business? The cactus varieties are your best bet. A reliable plant sitter (perhaps a family member, significant other, or neighbor) could broaden your options. If you are careless, your prince may well become a frog shortly after its homecoming.

Availability:

Most local home-improvement stores, supermarkets, and plant nurseries carry my plant favorites. If your favorites are unavailable at the time of your visit, ask the greenhouse manager whether they will include it in their next shipment of interior plants. Using this book, be sure to specify the exact species of plant you are looking for to ensure the correct match. The "botanical" name can be found in italics by each plant portrait, starting on the next page.

Affordability:

Can you afford the plant? Before answering, consider the following: the sacrifice of two fast-food combo meals (which none of us needs) would afford you the opportunity to purchase most medium-sized plants ($10.00 to $20.00). Should you have to replace the plant because of first-time misfortune (and bad things do happen to good plants), it's important to know that studies show some Americans have lived longer without fast food!

Need a gift for someone? The medium-sized plant will be far less expensive and last far longer than a bouquet of fresh flowers. And who needs another candle?

The next section profiles my favorite twenty interior plants in the low-, medium-, and high-light categories.

BABY'S TEARS

Helxine soleirolii

Also Known As: *Japanese Moss, Irish Moss* or *Mind-your-own-business*

Care: Easy

Humidity: Moderate

Temperature: 65 - 75°F

Fertilize: Monthly

Water: Keep soil moist

Growth Habit: Low, spreading

Height: 3 to 5 in.

Flowers: Tiny, difficult to see with the naked eye

The references to moss in the common names for this plant are well founded for a number of reasons. Firstly, baby's tears will thrive in damp and shady conditions, like moss. Secondly, as baby's tears grow and spread out into a carpet of green, it has the appearance of moss.

Baby's tears has tiny, tiny, tiny leaves no larger than one-fourth of an inch, that grow on thin, thread-like stems. The plant spreads out along the soil in the pot to form a dense mat of green. It looks like a carpet and can be trimmed into shape. In days past, this plant was used as a ground cover in conservatories.

There is also a variety called 'Argentea' that has silvery leaves. It serves as a wonderful contrast when planted as a ground cover for taller green plants. Keep it in check though, because it can take over the pot. Sometimes you will see this plant called helxine. It is the same plant.

GROWING TIPS

• These babes are super easy to propagate. Simply cut out a "divot" of the green mat and place on the surface of new soil. Pad it down gently and let it grow.

• This plant grows best in a shallow container.

• Amend the soil with sand to increase drainage.

• Keep the plant out of direct sunlight.

JON'S INTERIOR DESIGN TIPS

General: Baby's tears look a lot like Chia Pets. They can be trimmed into haircuts very easily. Plant in a sculptural pot with a face on the side and you will be amazed at how many people notice your unusual plant.

Children's Room: Plant a children's dish garden with baby's tears. Grow the plant around tiny figurines of animals, ballerinas, even dinosaurs. Let your children design the landscape themselves with some of their favorite stories and tales.

TRIVIA - Native to the Mediterranean and Italy, baby's tears are sometimes called the Corsican Curse, because they can be invasive when grown outdoors in warmer climates.

CAST IRON PLANT

Aspiristra elatior

Also Known As: *Bar Room Plant*

Care: Easy

Humidity: Moderate, but will tolerate dryer air

Temperature: 55 - 70°F

Fertilize: Monthly

Water: Let soil dry out between waterings

Growth Habit: Upright. Leaves grow vertically, then arch. Slow growing

Height: 24 to 30 in.

Flowers: Small, purple to brown flowers

If the name of this plant doesn't give you a hint as to its formidable survival skills, then obtaining one and seeing for yourself will. The cast iron plant is the archetype of Victorian parlor plants. But it was also found in bar rooms and taverns because it could easily tolerate these low-light, smoky, and dank spaces.

Their dark green leaves have a waxy surface that gives them the appearance that they have been polished. You can't beat that, easy and self-polishing. This is exactly why the cast iron plant is enjoying resurgence in popularity.

GROWING TIPS

• The cast iron plant will grow with little light and humidity. However, given a little bit of both, it will be spectacular.

• Wipe leaves free of dust once a month.

JON'S INTERIOR DESIGN TIPS

Edwardian: To recreate the masculine ambiance of a leather-chaired, smoking room, introduce a cast iron plant. It will add that old-English, clubby ambiance, as well as tolerate low-light conditions and cigar smoke.

Office Couture: Since this plant thrives on low light, you can decorate any small corner with a cast iron plant. It will add charm to your workspace.

TRIVIA - The flowers of the cast iron plant grow low, near the soil line. It is believed that snails pollinate the flowers.

CHINESE EVERGREEN

Aglaonema commutatum

Also Known As: *Painted Drop Tongue*

Care: Easy

Humidity: Medium to High

Temperature: 65 - 75°F

Fertilize: Monthly

Water: Keep soil moist at all times

Growth Habit: Bushy. Slow growing

Height: 3 ft.

Flowers: Small, spathe-like flowers on tall stems should be removed

There is nothing fussy about the Chinese evergreen. A tolerant beauty with formidable survival skills, it is one of the easiest plants to grow indoors. It features graceful, arching leaves that sport a variety of markings in white and cream. Leaves are spear-shaped and are attached along a long green stalk.

Most varieties remain bushy and full, and grow to 3 feet tall. Since it is slow growing, it can remain a contained and dependable specimen for years. Here are some of my favorite varieties. All are easy to grow and care instructions for each are the same. Leaf coloration and size are the main difference between these cultivated varieties: *A.* 'Silver Queen', *A.* 'Silver King', *A.* 'Emerald Beauty', *A.* 'Silver Bay', and *A.* 'Maryann.'

GROWING TIPS

- Plants like to be potbound.

- Mist a few times a week, especially if room is dry and warm.

- Keep out of direct sun.

- Never let the roots sit in water, as root rot can become a problem.

- Should leaves have gray spots, the plant likely sustained injury from the cold. Remove damaged leaves and relocate plant to a warmer room.

JON'S INTERIOR DESIGN TIPS

General: Chinese evergreens are delightfully easy to grow and can be placed anywhere in your home that is not extremely sunny. When they are small, they make great tabletop specimens. As they grow large, they can be used as architectural interest in the same way that you might use a fern. The Chinese evergreen looks exceptionally beautiful on a pedestal.

TRIVIA - Chinese evergreens will grow roots if a cutting is set in water for about six weeks. Place in soil to give birth to a new plant.

CORN PLANT

Dracaena fragrans

Care: Easy

Humidity: Low

Temperature: 65 - 75°F

Fertilize: Monthly

Water: Allow soil to dry out between waterings

Growth Habit: Upright on vertical stalk

Height: 6 ft. or higher

Flowers: Purple hanging clusters, highly fragrant. Generally on older and taller plants

The corn plant is one of our most familiar and beloved interior plants. Leaves can grow 3 inches wide and up to 3 feet in length. They grow atop a "stalk" and the resemblance to a corn plant is remarkable. The leaves not only have the same shape and coloration of a corn plant leaf, they also have the same texture. The leaves flop over in the same relaxed arching spray.

A commonly grown variety of corn plant called *D. f.* 'Massangeana' has a yellow stripe running down the center of its leaves. Oftentimes you will find this plant with its stalk chopped off and new foliage growing from the side of the stalk, just below the cut. This is done to keep the plant from hitting its head on the ceiling. It also creates a more lush plant with a silhouette perhaps a bit more interesting than before.

GROWING TIPS

- Repot every two years.

- Should brown spots appear on leaves, the plant may have been sunscorched. Move the plant to a low-light location.

- Keep leaves free of dust.

JON'S INTERIOR DESIGN TIPS

Contemporary: The upright and rigid stem of the corn plant can be a sculptural element in a room with clean lines.

Picnic Perfect: Are you in charge of the Fourth of July picnic decorations this year? Display a series of corn plants potted in red, white, and blue pots along the back of your serving table to create a stand of corn.

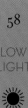

DIEFFENBACHIA

Dieffenbachia amoena

Also Known As: *Dumb Cane*

Care: Easy

Humidity: Moderate to high

Temperature: 60 - 80°F

Fertilize: Every two weeks in spring and summer. Monthly in fall and winter

Water: Keep soil slightly moist at all times

Growth Habit: Upright, tall or bushy

Height: 1 to 5 ft.

Flowers: Insignificant

One of the easiest of all interior plants to grow is the dieffenbachia. It is instantly recognizable by its big, showy, and sometimes variegated leaves. The dieffenbachia is a favorite of designers and often seen in furniture showrooms. It grows on thick canes that reach as high as 5 feet tall and can add beauty and color to a dimly lit corner of a room in minutes.

How can a plant be dumb, as this plant's alternate name suggests? It is due to the fact that the sap that seeps out from a plant cut is highly toxic. If it gets onto the mouth, lips, or tongue, it causes intense pain, leaving its victims unable to talk, rendering them "dumb." For this reason, one must be very careful when handling this plant and mindful of its placement in a room in which children and pets have access.

GROWING TIPS

- All parts of this plant are poisonous. Wear gloves when handling.

- Should tips of leaves become brown, make sure the plant is thoroughly watered, not just in a singular spot.

- Should leaves droop and wilt, water the plant immediately.

- Should leaves drop off while still appearing healthy, the plant may have been chilled. Move the plant to a warmer location.

- Repot every two to three years.

JON'S INTERIOR DESIGN TIPS

General: This winter, I put three small, 4-inch container plants in one round 1950s McCoy planter to make a beautiful centerpiece for my round coffee table.

Traditional: Dieffenbachia look at home in brass or metal planters. Be sure to place the plant inside a plastic container first before placing it inside a decorative metal container. This elegant plant can also look lovely in a planter with an Oriental motif.

Office Chic: Because they can stand low light, the dieffenbachia plant is a great fit for your office space, or consider them as a gift to a coworker or friend.

TRIVIA - The toxic substance in the leaves is very painful, but not deadly.

DWARF SCHEFFLERA

Heptapleurum arboricola

Care: Easy

Humidity: Moderate to high

Temperature: Average room temperature, 60 - 75°F

Fertilize: Monthly, except in winter months

Water: Keep soil slightly moist. Never allow roots to stand in water

Growth Habit: Bushy. Pinch tips back to retain shape

Height: Up to 6 ft. if not pinched back

Flowers: Insignificant

While high-light schaffleras grow 7 to 8 feet, the low-light dwarf schefflera grows commonly 2 to 3 feet, and as tall as 6 feet should the plant not be pinched back. On each plant, the leaves are the most distinctive feature. They are compound leaves with individual, elongated leaflets that grow in a circular pattern, creating a pinwheel effect. They are shiny and vivid green and grow on thin stems. Younger leaves have fewer leaflets, usually four to six. As the plant grows taller, the number of leaflets will increase to twelve to fourteen in number.

GROWING TIPS

- The dwarf schefflera will tolerate and thrive in higher-light conditions.

- Variegated varieties need a bit more light.

JON'S INTERIOR DESIGN TIPS

General: Use as a dense shrub to fill up empty, low-light areas, just as you would use the larger schefflera in high-light areas.

Color Splash: The variegated, yellow variety might complement a room decorated in brighter colors.

GOLDEN POTHOS

Epipremnum aureum

Also Known As: *Devil's Ivy*

Level of Care: Very easy

Humidity: Moderate

Temperature: Average room, 60 - 80°F

Fertilize: Every month

Water: Once a week, let dry out completely between waterings. Do not overwater

Growth Habit: Trailing. Fast growing

Height: Trailing vines up to 8 ft.

Flowers: Will not flower indoors

This is without a doubt one of the easiest of all interior plants to grow. It is tailor-made for the busy and the career minded, who may get around to watering their interior plants every now and then. While it won't thrive on neglect, it will survive. In fact, the only serious damage you can do to pothos is to overwater it.

The most distinguishing feature of golden pothos is its large, glossy leaves. They are heart-shaped and marbled with lemon-yellow color. There are other varieties like the 'Marble Queen', that has highly variegated leaves marbled with white. The leaves are abundant and grow on long trailing vines. Because of its similar characteristics it is easy to mistake it for a philodendron, which it is not, but to which it is closely related.

The golden pothos is a fast growing vigorous performer that is easy to incorporate into a home or office environment. They are reliable and tolerant. Many would consider them the most popular plant in the interior plant community.

GROWING TIPS

• Should leaves turn yellow and fall, cut back on water.

• It is tempting to let the vines grow as long as possible. Cut back once or twice a year to keep a neater, bushier shape.

• Staking to a moss pole or trellis will allow the vines to climb upward, increasing the height of the plant and showing off the heart- shaped leaves.

• This plant is so easy to care for that I will go out on a limb to say: "If you cannot handle golden pathos, you should consider taking up another hobby."

JON'S INTERIOR DESIGN TIPS

• Golden pothos make good hanging baskets.

• Grow this plant vertically by staking. Vines will form a nicely shaped specimen plant for the living room.

• Place atop tall pieces of furniture and allow vines to trail down.

TRIVIA - Golden pothos are used in industrial environments to help purify the air, particularly of formaldehyde.

GRAPE IVY

Cissus rhombifolia

Also Known As: *Begonia Vine*

Care: Easy

Humidity: Medium to high

Temperature: 55 - 70°F in winter; 65 - 80°F in summer

Fertilize: Monthly

Water: Keep soil moist in spring and summer. Allow plant to dry out slightly in fall and winter

Growth Habit: Vining, trailing. Fast growing

Height: 5 ft. or more

Flowers: Insignificant

Grape ivy is not really ivy at all. However, it is related to the grape family, which explains its tendrils that enable it to climb much like a vine. The beautifully shaped leaves easily bring to mind a rolling hillside of graceful vineyards. Here is the best interior plant for conjuring up a pastoral scene with an undemanding and fast-growing plant.

The leaves are lush and green and will thrive even in the dimmest of rooms. The bright green, triple leaflets are a rosy bronze color on the undersides, reminiscent of the colors of a vineyard in autumn.

GROWING TIPS

• Though this vine can grow up to 5 feet or more, it is best to keep pruned to 2 feet.

• Repot every spring. Use a porous potting mix for excellent drainage.

• Plant in hanging baskets on a moss pole or trellis, to support its vining habit.

• Should leaves turn brown at the tips, the humidity needs to be increased.

• Should leaves curl up on the ends, soil is to dry. Increase watering.

JON'S INTERIOR DESIGN TIPS

General: Grow these quaint and earthy vines in hanging baskets or in containers atop high armoires to allow them room to grow long and beautiful.

California Wine County: As a member of the grape family, there is literally no better vine to grow with your wine-country-inspired California scheme. They are at home in a gourmet kitchen, atop the pine cupboard or wine rack, or atop a wine barrel table in a dimly lit tasting room.

TRIVIA - Grape ivy is native to Central and South America.

LOW
LIGHT

KENTIA PALM

Howea forsteriana

Also Known As: *Sentry Palm*

Care: Easy

Humidity: Medium

Temperature: 60 - 80°F

Fertilize: Monthly

Water: Keep soil moist at all times. Allow to dry out between waterings in winter

Growth Habit: Upright, palm shapes on a single cane

Height: 8 ft.

Flowers: None

Kentia palms made their way to the west in about 1870, traveling from the Pacific islands off the coast of Australia. They became part of a group of palms that were known as the 'Palm Court' palms, because that is where they were most often planted, in Britain and eventually the States. For this purpose they are indeed ideal, as their feathery palms and moderate height are easily contained within large indoor landscapes.

H. Forsteriana is preferred in Britain. They have wider leaves and grow faster than *H. Belmoreana* preferred in America. Both are feathery, elegant and easy for which to provide care.

GROWING TIPS

• Most nurseries will sell this palm with multiple plants in each container. It is a very slow grower, so taller plants will cost more.

• Keep them cooler in the winter, especially at night. Temperatures as low as 60°F are ideal.

• Should frond tips turn brown, you may need to use pure water, as the kentia plant is very sensitive to chlorine and fluoride.

JON'S INTERIOR DESIGN TIPS

Edwardian Parlor: All palms are ideally suited for that old-fashioned Edwardian parlor look, but this one is particularly suited for it can stand low light.

TRIVIA - Kentia palms hail from Lord Howe Island, near Australia.

LADY PALM

Rhapis excelsa

Also Known As: *Little Lady Palm* or *Bamboo Palm*

Care: Easy

Humidity: Moderate

Temperature: 60 - 80°F

Fertilize: Monthly in spring and summer. Do not feed in winter

Water: Allow soil to dry out between waterings

Growth Habit: Bushy

Height: 10 ft.

Flowers: None

This is the classic palm tree that would have been grown by wealthy Americans in their conservatories around the turn of the century. Although originally from China, this palm came to the United States via Japan.

The fronds are exceptionally "Oriental" looking. They are fan shaped and consist of up to nine leaflets arranged in a palmate fashion. Each leaflet is about 1 inch in length. The ends of the leaflets are blunt, rather then pointy. It looks as if someone snipped off the ends with a pair of scissors.

One of the most unique features of the lady palm is its tendency to stay low and bushy, rather than tall and lanky. If a wonderful exotic and lush interior is one that you are trying to create, then the lady palm should be on your shopping list.

GROWING TIPS

- Repot every two years in a shallow pot.

- This plant can be grown as a bonsai. Although this plant can grow 10 feet in height, it is likely not to surpass the 3-foot mark given a small and shallow plant container.

- Keep soil mix light and porous to increase drainage.

JON'S INTERIOR DESIGN TIPS

Oriental: If you are trying to create an Oriental feeling, you can't beat this easy growing palm. Plant in a grouping with your Chinese or Japanese porcelain collection. The lady palm looks extremely attractive with blue and white English porcelain as well.

Party Festive: Brighten any celebration with this showy plant. Up-light with colored lights to create the appearance of bright, spectacular fire-works.

TRIVIA - There are more then 100 cultivars of this plant.

'LIME LIGHT' DRACAENA

Dracaena 'lime light'

Care: Easy

Humidity: Medium

Temperature: 65 - 70°F

Fertilize: Every two weeks

Water: Allow soil to dry out between waterings

Growth Habit: Vertical, then arching

Height: Can grow to 3 ft.

Flowers: Insignificant

Good low-light plants, especially those that will light up a room, are hard to find. This plant offers the pizzazz for which we have been waiting. The chartreuse color of the almost-electric 'lime light' dracaena is perhaps my favorite color outdoors (think sweet potato vine and coleus) as well my favorite apple (granny smith).

Its growth habit is long, lance-shaped leaves that grow in a fleur-de-lis pattern along a central, vertical stem. Common to most recently-introduced 'lime light' dracaena, 8 to 10 inch leaves eventually fall off from the bottom of the palm, exposing an attractive stem.

GROWING TIPS

• Should leaves fall off suddenly, the room may be too cold for the plant. Move the plant to a warmer location.

• Should leaves turn pale and colors fade, the plant may be undernourished or not getting enough light.

• Should leaves have brown spots, the plant may have been scorched from exposure to direct sunlight.

• The dracaena prefers to be potbound. Repot only every two or three years.

JON'S INTERIOR DESIGN TIPS

General: Despite its vibrant color, this plant and plant color seems oddly enough to complement all interior color selections. The color will brighten dimly lit rooms and dark corners.

MADAGASCAR DRAGON

Dracaena marginata tricolor

Care: Easy

Humidity: Medium

Temperature: 65 - 75°F

Fertilize: Monthly

Water: Allow soil to dry out between waterings

Growth Habit: Tall, upright

Height: 6 ft. or more indoors

Flowers: Insignificant

In its natural environment this dracaena can grow to 30 feet or more at maturity. It is a strikingly beautiful plant with spiky, striped green, cream, and pink foliage. Its unique growth habit is loosely tufted and branching. Young plants are commonly found with top to bottom foliage. With age, lower leaves tend to fall or can be trimmed back to expose its stem and an equally beautiful silhouette. In either presentation it makes for a noticeably bright and attractive interior plant.

GROWING TIPS

- Regular misting and a warm climate will keep this plant happy. The higher the room temperature, the higher its humidity requirements.

- Should leaf colors fade, increase the light.

- Should leaves turn all yellow and drop, decrease watering to prevent root rot.

JON'S INTERIOR DESIGN TIPS

General: Plant three plants of different height together in one large pot. This creates an interesting, three-tier arrangement that is quite pleasing.

Tabletop Gardens: Use small specimens of dracaena to add that upright element among lower growing dish gardens plants that have a vining or spreading habit.

MONEY TREE

Pachira aquatica

Also Known As: *Malabar Chestnut*

Care: Easy

Humidity: Moderate to high

Temperature: 65 - 75°F

Fertilize: Monthly

Water: Keep soil moist at all times. Mist foliage

Growth Habit: Upright with main "trunk." Tree-shaped

Height: Up to 6 ft. indoors

Flowers: Brush-shaped, white and red, never indoors

The money tree is one of the feng shui plants that is purported to bring wealth and prosperity to its owner, hence its name as the money tree. It is also a very attractive plant. Hey, count me in. I get to have a pretty house and make some extra cash? It's a win - win to say the least.

The leaves of the money tree are handsome. They have five leaflets per stem that form the shape of an open hand with five fingers. As the plant increases in height the leaves increase in size and become thicker and darker green. They tend to hang gently like parasols. In the wild they can grow to 60 feet in height. The money tree is a chestnut tree that can produce large, edible chestnuts the size of baseballs. As an interior plant they will not produce nuts or flowers.

Not only does the money tree bring good vibes, it is also amazingly easy to grow.

GROWING TIPS

- The natural habitat of the money tree is a swamp, or wetlands. Given their love for water, keep soil moist all the time.

- The bathroom, near a shower, is the perfect environment for this plant.

- While in direct sun, never let the leaves get wet to avoid leaf burn.

JON'S INTERIOR DESIGN TIPS

General: One of the very best ways to grow the money tree is as a single plant with a braided trunk. Plant in an exquisite pot elevated on an ebony or iron stand and place as a focal point in the room. It's outstanding as a tree.

Family Room Cozy: While the plant is smaller, keep it in plain view on a coffee table top. The leaves are lovely when viewed from eye level or above.

TRIVIA - The braided trunks of the money tree is a feng shui principle that is supposed to trap money in the crux of the braids.

MOTHER-IN-LAW'S TONGUE

Sansevieria trifasciata

Also Known As: *Snake Plant*

Care: Easy

Humidity: Low

Temperature: 65 - 75°F, and never below 60°F

Fertilize: Monthly. Half strength in winter

Water: Once a week

Growth Habit: Stiff, vertical. Slow growing

Height: 2 to 3 ft.

Flowers: Small, white spires. May occur on older plants

This sturdy plant has an iron clad reputation for being virtually indestructible. They will tolerate an enormous amount of neglect, unlike your mother-in-law. They will hang on, in the most miserable of conditions. The only thing that you can do to kill them is to water them to death. The mother-in-law's tongue is a succulent, meaning that its leaves are thick and store water, much like a cactus. Because of this feature, the tall sword-like leaves are turgid, stiff and very dramatic.

The only visible portion of this plant it its leaves. There are no visible stems. The sharply pointed leaves are variegated with a pattern reminiscent of snakeskin markings. The leaves have a slight twist to them, causing a pot of them to resemble a kelp garden, with its branches wavering in the under sea current.

GROWING TIPS

- Feel free to move this plant about the house. It tolerates relocation well.
- Don't allow water to settle in the center of the leaf rosette. It can cause rotting of the crown.
- Water moderately. Remember these plants grow wild under the South African sun.
- Keep roots restricted, but make certain the smaller pot is heavy enough to counter the heavy weight of the succulent leaves.

JON'S INTERIOR DESIGN TIPS

Industrial/Modern: Tall spiky plants create edgy excitement in a room as an exclamation mark does on paper!

Nautical: The subtle wavy growth habit of the leaves of the mother-in-law's tongue is complimentary to a nautical-inspired interior. Place near the aquarium to mimic seaweed. Set multiple pots in a row to create a living sculpture on a sofa table or shelf. Use as a backdrop to display your shell or coral collection.

TRIVIA - The mother-in-law's tongue is a natural air filter. It can absorb toxic substances from the air.

LOW LIGHT

NERVE PLANT

Fittonia verschaffeltii

Also Known As: *Silver Net Leaf*

Care: Moderate, but a bit sensitive

Humidity: High

Temperature: 65 - 75°F

Fertilize: Monthly

Water: Lightly and often. Keep soil moist. Never let soil dry out

Growth Habit: Creeping and vining tendencies. Trim to keep bushy

Height: 6 to 8 in.

Flowers: Small, yellow flowers. Should be removed

The beauty of the nerve plant is the intricate pattern of veins that lay across its leaves. The pattern is web-like and as detailed as a high-quality lace. Vein colors range from red to pink, to white and green. Each leaf is oval-shaped and grows on a fleshy stem in a trailing manner. For outstanding ornamental value, this plant is a stunner.

Temperamental, you say? Well, yes, this plant can be a bit sensitive. Mostly the nerve plant is affected by conditions that are cold and boggy, and has been known to basically drop dead, literally overnight, due to stress. So the secret is out, simply keep it warm and moist. The best way to do this is to keep nerve plant in a terrarium or bottle garden.

GROWING TIPS

• Nerve plants do not enjoy the cold, thus keep it away from drafts. Water this plant with warm water, not hot.

• If the leaves become bedraggled and straggly, give them a haircut to keep the plant in shape.

JON'S INTERIOR DESIGN TIPS

Terrarium: Nerve plants love dish gardens and terrariums. And the pizzazz that their patterned leaves add is invaluable. The leaves will stay small and contained, with an occasional need to be pinched back.

Contemporary: In a room void of patterned wallcoverings, furniture, or window-treatments, the never plant will introduce an organic element with geometric flair.

TRIVIA - The nerve plant is native to the forests of Peru where they creep across the forest floor like a beautiful, patterned carpet.

PARLOR PALM

Neanthe bella

Also Known As: *Dwarf Mountain Palm* or *Good Luck Palm*

Care: Easy

Humidity: Moderate to high. Mist often

Temperature: 65 - 80°F

Fertilize: Every two weeks

Water: Regularly. Keep soil moist

Growth Habit: Upright with arching palm fronds. Slow growing

Height: 3 to 4 ft., rarely will grow to 6 ft. indoors

Flowers: Only after three years of age

Parlor palms have long and graceful, arching fronds with thin, elongated leaves that one can easily imagine swaying to and fro in an island breeze. The plant fronds look fragile, but they are actually not. Parlor palm can withstand a little jostling without damage to their fronds. They are commonly used in high-traffic locations found in business offices and malls. As with all palms, the parlor palm is a native of the tropics; therefore warmth is its primary requisite for survival.

GROWING TIPS

• Parlor palms need to be kept moist.

They should never be allowed to dry out or allowed to stand in water. Excessively wet soil can lead to root rot.

• Palms grow best in warm conditions. Protect them from drafts.

JON'S INTERIOR DESIGN TIPS

Island Retreat: Use this exotic looking palm to evoke the serenity of a faraway location.

British Empire: The British colonial feel is easy to recreate with the addition of a parlor palm.

Cuban Cigar Bar: Sheer draperies, louvered blinds, overhead fan, an old photo of Hemingway, a parlor palm – these are room requirements if you're to make even Jimmy Buffet feel at home.

TRIVIA - In medieval fortune telling, it was considered the best of omens should you dream of palm trees.

PEACE LILY

Spathiphyllum wallisii

Also Known As: *Spath Flower* or *White Sails*

Care: Easy

Humidity: High

Temperature: 65 - 75°F

Fertilize: Monthly

Water: Keep soil moist

Growth Habit: Upright with outward arching leaves

Height: 18 in. to 5 ft.

Flowers: Showy, white, lily-shaped

This is a thirsty one. Should you enjoy a daily plant care regime for your indoor plants, the peace lily should definitely make your roster for future rounds.

Long, lance-shaped leaves that grow in a neat circular clump around a center are just one of the attractive features of this plant. The white, lily-like flowers that grow on long wiry stems are the main reason many introduce the peace lily to their family. The flower is long-lasting and rises above the foliage layer, bringing it stage forward in its display.

GROWING TIPS

• Keep this plant away from drafts.

• Repot every year.

• Remove spent flowers by cutting down supporting stems at their base.

• Should leaves wilt and then droop, water immediately. The plant will be revived within a short time. Repeat offenses will prove harmful to the peace lily.

• Should no flowers appear, move the plant to a brighter location.

JON'S INTERIOR DESIGN TIPS

Scientist Hip: Are you a teacher of anatomy and physiology with a lab filled with specimens preserved in formaldehyde-based solutions? Keep this plant around to filter the air, as well to cure student blues should exam results go south.

Spa: Particularly in the nail salon where toxic chemicals fill the air, invite the peace lily to improve air quality. Its beautiful and feminine flowers are also perfect for promoting a relaxing day at the spa.

TRIVIA - According to NASA, spaths can assist in cleaning the air of formaldehyde, carbon monoxide, and benzene.

PRAYER PLANT

Maranta leuconeura

Also Known As: *Husband and Wife Plant*

Care: Moderate

Humidity: High

Temperature: 65 - 80°F. Prefers warmth

Fertilize: Every two weeks in spring and summer. Cut back in winter.

Water: Keep soil moist in spring and summer. Water less in winter

Growth Habit: Bushy, with angular positioning of the leaves

Height: 12 in.

Flowers: Small, white flowers that are insignificant

The prayer plant is grown for its spectacular display of pattern and color on its foliage. The beautiful, oblong leaves are marked with distinct colorations to the midrib and veins, and patterns along the surface. Red, green, grey, and maroon are the most common colors. There are several varieties of prayer plants, each with nicknames that were obviously inspired by markings on their leaves. 'Rabbit Tracks' has a pattern that resembles brown rabbit prints between the veins. The herringbone plant displays bright red veins in an intricate, herringbone pattern.

Prayer plants have shallow roots and like to be grown in low pots. The plant will eventually grow wider than it is tall, approximately 12 inches tall by 16 inches wide.

The common name of this plant is related to its unique ability to fold up its leaves similar to hands in prayer. This happens in response to darkness. Leaves will open up in the morning. Some people claim to hear a fluttering noise as these leaves unfurl.

GROWING TIPS

• Given a shallow root system, the prayer plant prefers a shallow container.

• Leaves are produced only during the growing season. They "rest" during autumn and winter.

JON'S INTERIOR DESIGN TIPS

Bathroom Retreat: Warm, humid conditions near your shower or soaking tub make ideal homes for the prayer plant.

Dish Garden: Plant in a shallow dish garden with other humidity-loving plants. Place on a pebble dish for a spa-like ambiance.

TRIVIA - On the *Mary Tyler Moore Show*, Lou receives a prayer plant as a gift and replies, "I'll try not to swear in front of it."

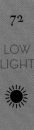

LOW
LIGHT

STRIPED DRACAENA

Dracaena deremensis 'Warneckii'

Also Known As: *Ribbon Plant*

Care: Easy

Humidity: Low to medium

Temperature: 65 - 75°F

Fertilize: Every two weeks in spring and summer; monthly in winter and fall

Water: Allow soil to dry out between waterings

Growth Habit: Central stem, upright. Slow growing

Height: 4 ft. or more

Flowers: Insignificant

The striped dracaena is the slowest growing of all dracaena. This is not a bad attribute, especially for an indoor plant. As a result, the plant is able to retain a fuller shape longer. It will eventually grow in height, while the main stem begins to elongate similar to other dracaena varieties. This stem transformation will take place over a period of years.

The striped dracaena is the most common and most attractive variety. Its leaves are striped in two shades of green. This plant grows in low-light conditions and can tolerate drier air and soil than most. The deep, green leaves are long, sword-shaped, and can reach a foot and a half in length.

GROWING TIPS

- Repot every two to three years
- Looks best when three to five stalks are planted in a single planter.
- Keep leaves free of dust.
- To prevent leaves from burning, never place the plant in direct sunlight.

- Should the plant's lowest leaves begin to fall off, the plant may be too cold. Increase room temperature.

JON'S INTERIOR DESIGN TIPS

General: The dracaena is grown primarily for its form. It performs best and most often solo.

ZZ PLANT

Zamioculcas zamiifolia

Care: Easy

Humidity: Low

Temperature: 65 - 75°F

Fertilize: Monthly

Water: Let soil dry out between waterings

Growth Habit: Spiky

Height: 18 to 24 in.

Flowers: Yellow-brown spath

The zz plant is grown for its exquisite, pinnate foliage with leaves that are dark green and shiny as a boxwood. Leaves are held on a sturdy stem that grow out from the tubers that lie just below the soil surface. The entire shape of the plant is much like that of a feathery palm, though it is not a palm at all.

This plant does not have an official "also known as name," but when it does attain a few nicknames, the list is likely to include "Easy zz" because it is quite possibly the easiest interior plant to maintain. It has basically two requirements, water and light, and neither is required in large quantity. You can literally ignore this plant for weeks and it will survive.

Perhaps the only "not easy" thing about this plant is locating it. Today,

it isn't yet readily available at all the regular hand-outs. You might look first at upscale garden centers or order it online to avoid a game of hide-and-seek. I am comfortable you will find this plant to be well worth the extra effort.

GROWING TIPS

Caution All parts of the zz plant are poisonous.

- Should leaves turn yellow, the plant may be overwatered.

- Do not use leaf shine products on the leaves of the zz plant.

JON'S INTERIOR DESIGN TIPS

General: This is the best in show plant for some time. It is certain to catch

on as a popular interior plant. Use it in the interior much in the same way you would use a palm. Otherwise focus on its upright, statuesque, and distinct manner as an architectural feature.

Children's Room: Treat your teenagers to a zz plant with tails of thick, spear-shaped leaves resembling the jagged backs of their favorite prehistoric dinosaurs.

TRIVIA - The zz plant is native to Zanzibar.

AFRICAN VIOLET

Saintpaulia ionantha

Care: Easy to moderate

Humidity: High

Temperature: 65 - 75°F

Fertilize: Every two weeks

Water: Water only when the top of soil is dry. Do not allow water to touch plant leaves

Growth Habit: Circular

Height: 6 to 8 in.

Flowers: Beautiful, long-lasting blossoms in reds, pinks, violets, blues, purples, and white

The African violet has a reputation for being an extraordinary beauty, but a bit fussy. While they have specific watering requirements, the latter description is perhaps a slight exaggeration. It's important to note that newer hybrids are remarkably more tolerant of fluctuating living conditions than those with which you grew up.

We keep African violets for their bright abundant flowers that grow as if a florist has delicately arranged them. They are set in the center of a circular bed of fuzzy green leaves resembling a bridal bouquet. The entire arrangement seldom grows taller then eight inches and is one of the most delightful and beloved of all flowering interior plants.

The story goes that a WWI soldier from Germany found violet specimens and sent them to Europe, where they were studied. It was found that the violet was a plant unknown to Europe at the time. The soldiers's name was Saint Paul; the Latin name saintpauli reflects this link.

GROWING TIPS

• Purchase an African violet pot for best results. These pots are specially designed to facilitate watering by way of a double pot, one that fits inside of the other. Their design allows the leaves of the African violet to lay over the rim of the pot, while high and dry above wet soil.

• For ideal growing conditions, African violets require light for 8 to 12 hours per day. Given less light than required, the leaves will darken.

• African violets should not be exposed to direct sunlight.

JON'S INTERIOR DESIGN TIPS

Victorian: Any proper Victorian lady or gentleman would have appreciated the perfect growing habit and the bright delicate flowers of the African violet. The circular growth of the African violet resembles a nosegay that Victorian women were known to have carried.

Romantic: Liven up a lady's dressing table or place near a lace-covered window of a parlor.

Modern: Jaunty and colorful African violets will be stunning in pots of primary colors.

ALUMINUM PLANT

Pilea cadierei

Also Known As: *Watermelon Pilea*

Care: Easy

Humidity: Moderate to high

Temperature: Average room temperature, 60 - 75°F

Fertilize: Monthly

Water: Keep soil moist, never allowing roots to stand in water

Growth Habit: Bushy, fast growing

Height: 12 in.

Flowers: Tiny white flowers

MEDIUM LIGHT

The leaves of the aluminum plant are unusual, possessing a unique quilted texture. The raised surfaces of the leaves are a striking silver color, hence its name. Each leaf has four linear rows of upraised silver patches. The pattern resembles the markings on the rind of a watermelon, giving it the alternate name, watermelon pilea. The leaves are about 3 inches long and are borne on attractive pink stems that eventually become woody.

GROWING TIPS

• The aluminum plant will grow very well in hanging baskets.

• Plants naturally tend to get leggy; therefore pinch leaves back to produce bushier growth.

• The aluminum plant will thrive in the warm, humid air of a terrarium or under a glass cloche (bell jar).

JON'S INTERIOR DESIGN TIPS

General: Since aluminum plants like shallow containers, and since the leaf pattern is so beautiful when viewed from above, it is best suited as a table-top specimen.

Country: The quilt-like surfaces of the leaves mix nicely with homespun patterns and textures. Grow in an "aluminum" watering can and set on the shady side of the sleeping porch to create the perfect summertime vignette.

Office: Aluminum plants are traditionally small, therefore easy to enjoy on the corner of a work desk or in a cubicle without getting in the way. The silver color coordinates nicely with most high-tech office environments.

TRIVIA - The aluminum plant is native to Vietnam.

ANTHURIUM

Anthurium hybrids

Also Known As: *Flamingo Flower*

Care: Moderate

Humidity: High

Temperature: 65 - 80°F

Fertilize: Monthly with high phosphorus fertilizer to encourage blooms

Water: Keep soil moist at all times

Growth Habit: Upright

Height: 12 to 18 in.

Flowers: Red, pink, white, and orange

The bloom of the anthurium, reminiscent of the tropics, is often used as a cut flower. It is usually seen in a bright red color with a central tail-like object. This "tail" is called a spadix, which is really a column made up of many tiny flowers. The red portion, called a spathe, is actually a covering that protects the spadix. But for now let's just call the entire structure a "flower."

Flowers on the anthurium are shiny and waxy and are shaped quite like an artist's palette. They often grow to more than 4 inches in length. Their beauty is extended over a long period of time, as the flowers can live for two months. Newer hybrids are capable of blooming several times in one year.

When the anthurium is not in bloom, the foliage, which mimics the palette shape of its flowers in some cases, is also quite remarkable. Some varieties have striations and silver veins, while others are a bit more heart-shaped and deep green in color. If that is not enough drama, the leaves often reach 7 inches in length. This plant is more expensive than many other interior plants, but their impact on a room is well worth the extra cost.

GROWING TIPS

Caution Prevent pets from chewing on leaves to avoid a burning sensation in their mouths.

• Keep away from drafts and drastic changes in temperature.

• Keep leaves free of dust by spraying with lukewarm water. Wipe gently, as their leaves are sensitive.

• Should the long tail in the middle of the flower begin to drop pollen and become messy, it can be cut off from its base without hurting the flower.

• When potting, use African violet soil mix. It is the perfect growing medium.

• Should the anthurium fail to bloom, the plant is either too young or in need of additional hours of light.

JON'S INTERIOR DESIGN TIPS

Tropical Fever: There are so many tropical interior plants from which to choose. Many are striking and exotic. The anthurium's hot color palette of bright red and orange is far from trendy: it is culturally evocative, especially if you are incorporating Mexican and Cuban elements into your living space.

ARROWHEAD VINE

Syngonium podophyllum

Care: Easy

Humidity: Moderate

Temperature: 60 - 90°F, 70°F is best

Fertilize: Every two weeks

Water: Keep soil moist, not drenched

Growth Habit: Upright, vining

Height: 12 to 15 in.

Flowers: None

Upon examination of the arrowhead vine one will notice an odd feature: its leaves are shaped differently and vary in shades of green. Dark green juvenile leaves are shaped like arrowheads, while newer leaves introduce a softer heart-shape and the color of lime green. As the plant matures, evolution of its leaves continues. Mature leaves have five lobes and resemble the shape of a maple leaf. Supporting stems of the larger leaves are weaker than the supporting stems of the juvenile leaves, and thus may require staking. At this point, the vining habit becomes evident. The resulting specimen is one that is truly unique, featuring on the same plant leaves of different size, shape, color, and supporting branch. There are varieties now available that are more colorful, including shades of bronze and light pink.

GROWING TIPS

- Should leaves become pale in color, they may be receiving too much sunlight.

- Should leaves appear to dry up and turn brown, your plant may have been damaged from chemicals in the environment, pesticides, smoke, or leaf cleaning products. Rinse leaves thoroughly in an effort to remove chemical residues.

- Should newer leaves turn brown, the plant is likely thirsty. Increase water.

- Keep this plant out of doorways where drafts can harm it.

JON'S INTERIOR DESIGN TIPS

General: The beauty of the arrowhead is its versatile foliage. While it's a strong, upright specimen in its youth, its true nature as a vine becomes evident as it matures. It can be trained to adhere to a moss pole or trellis for a vertical effect, or can be hung in a basket and allowed to trail freely.

Terrariums: The arrowhead vine is not the first plant most terrarium aficionados think of when creating a miniature garden. It does, however, make a perfect specimen as it can create height when planted with low-growing creepers. Use baby plants, of course.

TRIVIA - Since the 1850s, the arrowhead vine has had approximately twenty-five botanical names.

ASPARAGUS FERN

Asparagus setaceus

Also Known As: *Emerald Fern, Emerald Feather,* or *Foxtail Fern*

Care: Easy

Humidity: High

Temperature: 60 -75°F

Fertilize: Every two weeks with a standard blend

Water: Keep soil moist

Growth Habit: Trailing

Height: 24 in.

Flowers: Small, white. Sporadic blooming habit

Despite a misleading introduction, this member of the lily family is not a fern at all. However, I have included it among my fern favorites in this book, given similar plant qualities and likely use.

The asparagus from your vegetable garden (after the spears have been harvested and eaten), very much resemble asparagus fern. The long and delicate, needle-like leaves of both plants look very similar. And, in fact, both plants are related. However, do not try to dine on any part of the asparagus fern. It is not edible.

You most certainly have noticed this plant's leaves in florist bouquets. It is the flat, stiff fern-like leaf that appears to have been pressed. It is lacy and delicate, and makes for a most alluring interior plant.

GROWING TIPS

• There are tiny thorns growing among the leaves. Be careful when handling.

• Display in a hanging basket.

• Watch room humidity closely. Mist often in warmer temperatures.

• Should leaves drop, decrease room temperature.

JON'S INTERIOR DESIGN TIPS

General: I love ferns. I would venture to say that like the British fern collectors, I too am an erudite fan of this most humble of prehistoric forest dwellers. I was nearly eye level with the wispy fronds of the first fern that I ever saw.

Walking through the woods with my father nearly every day of my boyhood taught me to value and appreciate the beauty and respect the character of the magical fern. I often incorporate them into my garden designs, outdoors and in. They have a soothing effect in every location. They are especially beautiful and happy in bathrooms.

BIRD'S NEST FERN

Asplenium nidus

Also Known As: *Spleenwort*

Care: Moderate

Humidity: Medium, but will tolerate dryer air

Temperature: 55 - 75°F

Fertilize: Monthly from spring to fall. Monthly at half strength in winter

Water: Maintain constantly moist soil. Let dry out in winter

Growth Habit: Vase-shaped, slow

Height: 18 in. to 2 ft.

Flowers: None

The bird's nest fern is a bold, broad-leaved plant that makes a big statement. Its long fronds have a luxurious shine and are lightly ruffled on the edges. They arch gracefully, creating a vase-shaped silhouette that is quite elegant. There is a distinct beauty to the color of the fronds, light green chartreuse that is reminiscent of a granny smith apple. As the plant matures, the midribs of the fronds become a dark brown color, further emphasizing the striking green color.

The bird's nest fern also has another, most charming feature. The fronds grow in a rosette pattern from a central crown located at the soil line in the center of the plant. The crown is brown and hairy and looks like a bird's nest. When the new leaves emerge from the crown, they are a light shade of green and look like little eggs sitting in the nest. It is a lovely little surprise, one that will delight children of all ages.

GROWING TIPS

- Keep leaves free of dust. Be very careful when cleaning the youngest leaves, for they do not like to be handled.

- Repot every two years, preferably in the spring.

- Older fronds may turn brown. Cut them off at the base with clean, sharp scissors.

JON'S INTERIOR DESIGN TIPS

Spa Bathroom: Most ferns would be at home in a bright modern bathroom. Create an oasis that is light and airy, delicate, and peaceful. Who doesn't need a calm place to de-stress?

TRIVIA - In olden days, this fern used to be called a spleenwort because it was believed to cure ailments associated with the spleen. Do not try this at home, folks.

BRAKE FERN

Pteris cretica

Also Known As: *Table Fern* or *Ribbon Fern*

Care: Easy

Humidity: Moderate to high

Temperature: 60 - 70°F

Fertilize: Every week with diluted standard fertilizer

Water: Keep soil moist at all times

Growth Habit: Slow

Height: 6 to 12 in., can reach 36 in. in ideal conditions

Flowers: None

The fronds of this unusual plant do not resemble any other fern. The leaflets are spaced wide apart, atop long bare stalks. There are up to five leaflets on a single stalk, with the middle one being longer then the rest. The edges are delicately laced, creating a fringed appearance. When leaflets are fully grown, they elongate and look much like a ribbon just unfurled from its roll.

They make lovely additions to dish gardens or terrariums. They shine as a centerpiece on a dining table, especially when mixed with flowering plants as the unique leaf structure stands out in contrast.

GROWING TIPS

- Plant foliage is somewhat stiff and fragile, therefore avoid plant placement in high traffic areas.

- As its nickname (table fern) might suggest, this plant is best suited for growing in a standard pot on a table, not from a hanging basket. Repot every year.

- Mist often in warmer rooms.

JON'S INTERIOR DESIGN TIPS

Classic Kitchen: Elegant kitchen designs featuring brushed nickel, black and white floors, granite, hardwoods, or stainless steel will benefit from the soft flowing brightness that a fern will bring to the design.

ELEPHANT'S EAR

Alocasia sanderiana

Also Known As: *Kris Plant*

Care: Moderate

Humidity: Moderate

Temperature: 65 - 75°F

Fertilize: Every two weeks

Water: Keep soil evenly moist

Growth Habit: Spiky

Height: 30 to 36 in.

Flowers: Small flowers that should be removed

MEDIUM LIGHT

The leaves on this plant, as one might suspect, are enormous, like giant floppy elephant ears. Measuring 1 to 2 feet long, they hang from thick stems, and are immediately recognizable. Some leaves have a silvery, grey color to their veins. Other varieties have contrasting white veins. Both are sensational and theatrical. Certainly, they are the focal point of any room in which they are introduced.

GROWING TIPS

Caution: While it might be tempting to use this plant to create a jungle atmosphere in a child's space, note that the plant is highly poisonous and the sap can cause severe dermatitis.

- This plant likes to rest in the winter. Water less and fertilize less during its time off.

- Mist the giant leaves frequently.

- Do not wipe the leaves.

- Repot once a year in spring.

JON'S INTERIOR DESIGN TIPS

Groovy: If you're looking for a plant with hip making abilities, this is the ticket. Think of planters in bright colors, beaded doorways, black lights, lava lamps. You get the picture.

Tropical: Being a native to the tropics, it almost goes without saying that this specimen would fit into a tropically detailed room or greenhouse.

TRIVIA - The elephant's ear is native to the Philippines.

ENGLISH IVY

Hedera helix

Care: Easy

Humidity: Moderate

Temperature: 50 - 70°F

Fertilize: Monthly with a high nitrogen fertilizer

Water: Allow soil to dry out slightly between waterings. Best to water often and lightly

Growth Habit: Trailing vine, fast

Height: 6 to 8" as a houseplant. Can grow longer in ideal conditions

Flowers: Small greenish white, appearing in fall

There are many interior plants that are often referred to as "ivy." However, only one, the *Hedera helix* or English ivy, is the "true" ivy to which we are most accustomed. This is the ivy you've seen in historic homes and estates in Europe – the one that covers brick walls and arbors with beautiful blankets of green. As an interior plant, the English ivy could indeed crawl up walls, clinging to wallpaper and molding. Despite its appeal, especially to the kids, it is best perhaps to keep this plant confined to a pot.

There are many, many varieties of English ivy from which to choose. There are varieties that feature leaves variegated with yellows, creams, and whites. Leaf shapes can vary from simple shields to multiple lobed star shapes. One of the most intriguing varieties is a miniature called *H. Helix* 'Mini Ester' that presents tiny, frosted, green leaves perfect for interior plant lovers.

The best characteristic of English ivy is that it is very tolerant of cool temperatures. In fact, it prefers them to warm temperatures. It is logical to place this plant near doorways or cool windows. Since there are not many interior plants that can tolerate those conditions, this true ivy is a real keeper.

GROWING TIPS

Caution The sap of English ivy is poisonous and can cause dermatitis to the skin. The leaves are poisonous.

• Should the room temperature rise higher then 65 – 70°F, the chance for spider mites and aphids increases.

• Repot every one to two years.

• Should leaf tips turn brown, the air might be too dry. Mist often.

• Should new growth appear undersized and sparse, increase plant exposure to light.

• Should variegated leaves appear mostly green, increase light to promote brighter colors.

JON'S INTERIOR DESIGN TIPS

General: The English ivy's affection for cool temperatures makes it a perfect choice for an entryway table.

Topiary: Should you wish to grow a living vine on a moss-filled topiary form, the English ivy is the plant to use. English ivy grows quickly and is easy to maintain.

GINGER

Alpinia zerumbet 'variegata'

Also Known As: *Variegated Shell Ginger* or *Variegated Shellflower*

Care: Moderate

Humidity: High

Temperature: 60 – 75°F

Fertilize: Monthly

Water: Keep soil moist, never soggy

Growth Habit: Upright

Height: 3 to 4 ft.

Flowers: White and pink. Rarely flowers

Most gingers are grown for their large exotic flowers. This one is not. The *Alpinia zerumbet* is grown for its show-stopping foliage. A very beautiful variegated pattern is borne on leaves that have a uniquely elongated oblong shape. They grow in a spiral pattern outward from the crown. The deep green leaves are streaked with bright yellow and make a most beautiful specimen that is sure to garner attention, no matter where you place it.

This plant is not always easy to find, but, like the zz plant, is becoming more prevalent as gardeners become aware of its outstanding characteristics.

GROWING TIPS

• Keep in mind that blooms will not appear on a young plant. Other varieties of ginger are grown for their flowers. This plant is grown for its outstanding foliage.

• Ginger likes bright light, but never direct sunlight.

• Keep plant in a cooler place during the winter.

JON'S INTERIOR DESIGN TIPS

General: Ginger grows in beautiful, lush clumps. A single pot is oftentimes all that you need to create a striking look. In fact, because of their bright patterned leaves, too many plants placed together will likely prove too busy.

Raised Pot: Grow a single specimen in a raised planter about 3 feet tall. It will allow admirers a bird's-eye view of this plant's beautiful foliage along with the spiraling pattern of its leaves.

TRIVIA - Although native to Southeast Asia, the ginger plant was named after an Italian botanist from the seventeenth century named Prospero Alpini.

GOLDFISH PLANT

Nematanthus wettsteinii

Care: Moderate

Humidity: High

Temperature: 65 - 75°F

Fertilize: Monthly

Water: Let soil dry out very slightly between waterings

Growth Habit: Upright with arching stems

Height: 3 ft.

Flowers: Orange, red, tubular flowers

We've all heard different goldfish stories: "I bought a goldfish and it died in two weeks," or "I've had this fish forever. It just keeps growing." This gamut of sentiment is expressed regarding the care of the goldfish plant as well. Some people think they are easy to care for, while others seem to have no luck in growing them at all. If you are up for it, I believe it is worth the gamble.

This plant is truly striking. Goldfish-shaped, orange flowers dangling from the ends of arched stems create the illusion of fish leaping from a stream. The oval leaves of this plant have russet-colored hairs that give them a coppery appearance, not unlike the scales of a fish. The stems grow upward and then arch over the side of the container, thus making them ideal in hanging baskets. Stems can trail up to 3 feet in length.

GROWING TIPS

• The goldfish plant is related to the African violet, thus an African violet soil blend is an ideal growing medium.

• Should leaves suddenly drop, the plant is too cold.

• The real trick is balancing humidity and water. Keep air moist, and water regularly. Never let the soil get soggy.

JON'S INTERIOR DESIGN TIPS

General: Children's rooms are the ideal place to grow a goldfish plant in a hanging basket. They will have fun finding names for each and every goldfish.

TRIVIA - The goldfish plant is a native of Cost Rica.

HEART-LEAF PHILODENDRON

Philodendron scandens

Also Known As: *Sweetheart Plant* or *Heart-Leaf Philodendron*

Care: Easy

Humidity: Moderate

Temperature: 60 - 70°F

Fertilize: Monthly. In winter cut back every six weeks

Water: Allow soil to dry out slightly. Never let the plant get "bone dry"

Growth Habit: Vining, loves to climb

Height: 4 to 5 ft.

Flowers: Insignificant

The heart-leaf philodendron is the perfect example of a vining interior plant. It may look dainty with pretty, glossy, heart-shaped leaves rarely growing more than 2 inches in length, but is instead rather tough, resilient even in less than ideal conditions. It is a talented athlete, a gymnast to be exact. It can be trained to climb up, down, or sideways. It is happiest when it has a strong support that allows it to perform.

GROWING TIPS

• Either grow this athlete in a hanging basket or in a pot along with a moss pole or trellis for it to climb up.

Attach the stems of the plant to the pole with florist tape or twist ties. The aerial roots of the plant will take over from there.

• Repot every two years, being careful not to break the stems that are attached to the pole.

• You can keep as a hanging basket also. Cut back stems often to maintain a fuller appearance.

• Keep leaves free of dust to prevent spider mites.

• Give the plant a shower every few months to refresh it.

JON'S INTERIOR DESIGN TIPS

Bathroom Cool: Drape the vines of the Heart-leaf philodendron from a shelf above the entrance to your walk-in shower to create a jungle atmosphere. Your efforts are sure to make pre-bedtime clean-up for your children a bit more enjoyable.

HOLLY FERN

Cyrtomium falcatum

Also Known As: *Japanese Holly Fern*

Care: Easy

Humidity: Moderate, but can tolerate dryer conditions then most ferns

Temperature: 65 - 80°F, but can tolerate lower temperatures (50 – 70°F) in the winter

Fertilize: Weekly

Water: Keep soil lightly moist

Growth Habit: Loose and airy, shrubby. Long-lived

Height: 24 in.

Flowers: None

There are not many ferns that one would describe as "tough." But this is one of them. The holly fern is easy to care for and exceptionally tolerant of its living arrangements. All in all it is a very good roommate, and a handsome one at that.

The deep green leaves are sharply pointed on the ends and have jagged edges, much like the Christmas holly. The fronds can grow up to 2 feet long and form a long sweeping and arching branch. And since the fronds are stiffer than those found on most ferns, they are sturdier, but still have that magical airy fern quality, without all the fuss.

GROWING TIPS

• Plant several plants together in one pot for a fuller look.

• This plant can tolerate drafts better then most ferns, therefore better suited for entryways.

• Keep this plant's crown slightly above the soil line.

• Keep the holly fern away from bright sunlight.

• Repot every spring.

JON'S INTERIOR DESIGN TIPS

General: I love to use this plant in entryways and foyers. It mixes with nearly any kind of interior design scheme, and it is not fussy at all about frequent drafts from ongoing activity in and out of nearby doors.

TRIVIA - Holly ferns can survive temperatures as low as 30°F.

LADY SLIPPER ORCHID

Paphiopedilum

Also Known As: *Paph*

Care: Easy to moderate

Humidity: Moderate to high

Temperature: Day 70 - 85°F; night 55 - 60°F

Fertilize: Weekly

Water: Keep potting mixture moist at all times

Growth Habit: Slow

Height: 5 to 18 in.

Flowers: Uniquely shaped blossoms with "pouches." Long lasting

The most striking feature of this type of orchid is its rather flamboyant flowers. Usually the plant will send up one flower atop a single stalk. It has a predominant lip or pouch on the bottom with an upside down heart-shaped petal on the top. The striations of colors on the petal are intricate and opulent. They have a surreal quality to them, resembling a creature that is part bird and part insect. In some cases they resemble bats. The dramatic colorations are in hues of pink, brown, green, carmine, and white. There are even shades of deep mahogany. The markings on the flowers are sometimes solid, but some of the more exotic ones feature stripes and speckles in deeply contrasting colors.

One might think that the more exotic the flower appears, the more difficult it is to grow. This is not true. The lady slipper orchid is one of the easiest orchids to grow. It is perfect for a beginner, easy and showy. How fortuitous for those of us who like to show off every now and then.

GROWING TIPS

- The lady slipper orchid needs less light then other orchids, but still requires brighter light than most other indoor interior plants.

- There exists mottled leaf and solid green leaf lady slipper orchids. As a rule of thumb, the mottled leaf plants like warmer temperatures than the solid green leaf varieties.

- Add a pinch of lime to potting mixture to decrease acidity.

- Show off one single plant as a specimen in your finest pottery vase.

JON'S INTERIOR DESIGN TIPS

General: Orchids can be used in variety of ways to enhance the decoration of your home or workspace. Orchids can be formal, casual, tropical, and exotic, as well as historically emotive. I cannot think of another species of plants, beside ferns, that can add so much to an interior design scheme.

Asian Spa: This almost goes without saying. Since tropical motifs are all the rage presently, it is not difficult to imagine. Mix in with your rattans and bamboo for a serene setting.

MOTH ORCHID

Phalaenopsis

Also Known As: *Malaysian Flower*

Care: Easy to moderate

Humidity: High

Temperature: Day 75 - 85°F; night 60 - 65°F

Fertilize: "Weakly, weekly"

Water: Keep soil moist. Do not overwater

Growth Habit: Upright with arching stalks

Height: 15 to 24 in.

Flowers: Flat faced with colored centers; pink, white, and yellow. Long-lasting

The moth orchid is to many, the easiest of all orchids to grow indoors. They prefer moderate, indirect light, and thrive in the warmth of a well-heated room. These requirements are easily achievable in the average home environment.

The flowers on the moth orchid are large and very brightly colored. They have three distinct lobes on their lower lip. The center of the blossom is very erotic in its form and is often colored vivid red, purple, pink, or golden yellow. The moth orchid is also relatively inexpensive to purchase.

GROWING TIPS

• Repot every two years.

• The root system is very substantial. Keep them potbound.

• Should room temperature climb higher then 80°F, not to worry, simply increase humidity.

• Because the moth orchid cannot store water, they must be watered often. Monitor carefully, as the roots must also be able to dry out before the next watering to prevent root rot.

• Should leaves appear limp, do not water. Instead increase humidity.

JON'S INTERIOR DESIGN TIPS

British Colonial: A perfect contrast to the rich dark woods of the rainforest, or the mahoganies that the British used to create furniture that was reminiscent of home.

Modern: Use a single specimen to highlight or echo other architectural features.

TRIVIA - In their native habitat of the rain forest, moth orchids are often found growing on trees that hang overwater.

NORFOLK ISLAND PINE

Araucaria heterophylla

Also Known As: *Norfolk Pine*

Care: Easy

Humidity: Moderate to high

Temperature: 55 - 75°F

Fertilize: Monthly

Water: Keep soil moist

Growth Habit: Tall, upright, tree form. Slow

Height: 6 ft. or taller, to 100 ft. in native habitat

Flowers: None

Norfolk Island pines are ubiquitous during the holiday season, often given as predecorated gifts from the florist or even by mail order. And they do indeed make lovely presents, with tiny ornaments hanging from their soft, horizontal branches. Unfortunately, once the season is over, they are sadly parked on the curb with a stray piece of garland hanging off their bare branches, next to the wilted poinsettias.

This is unfortunate, as the Norfolk Island pine is not a difficult interior plant. It needs cooler temperatures than one might think; therefore do not place it next to the roaring holiday fire, even if it seems like the perfect spot. Instead, place it as far away from obvious heat sources as you can. Locate it near a bright, cool window. Mist it lightly every day if the house is dry from the heated air. It will thank you for it, and most likely live to see another holiday.

GROWING TIPS

• Should tips appear yellow or scorched, decrease fertilizer strength.

• Should branches droop, move the plant to a brighter location.

• Turn the plant often to encourage even growth.

JON'S INTERIOR DESIGN TIPS

Lodge Look: If you like the look of a lodge, these are just the ticket with deer antlers, chandeliers, and wooden beams.

PONYTAIL PALM

Beaucarnea recurvata

Care: Moderate

Humidity: Low

Temperature: 65 - 75°F

Fertilize: Monthly in spring and summer. Do not feed in winter

Water: Let soil dry out. Do not overwater in winter

Growth Habit: Upright, palm tree shaped. Very slow growing

Height: 6 to 8 ft.

Flowers: Small, white flowers on mature plants

This native to Mexico is an ideal interior plant. It is a desert dweller by birth and can tolerate the dry, overheated air of the modern home. It features a bulbous stem that is grayish brown in color. It looks like an elephant foot. This bulb is actually a water storage facility that allows this plant to tolerate dry conditions.

Atop the trunk-like stem is a loose sheaf of long strappy foliage. The plume of bright green leaves will grow only on the top of the "trunk." As the plant height increases, the leaves grow bushier and longer, but they will always stay in a clump at the very top of the stem, or stems.

The ponytail palm is a wonderful plant with which to associate. It has all the characteristics of a delightful companion. When it is young, it is charming and lovable. As it ages it becomes dignified and noble. The ponytail palm lives a very long time. No tearful good-byes.

GROWING TIPS

- The ponytail palm is slow growing, but if well taken care of, can live for thirty years or more.

- A balanced watering regime is perhaps the trickiest of care requirements. Do not overwater, and be careful of letting the soil get too dry. Try to establish a routine.

- Should the bulbous stem show softened or dark spots, stem rot is usually the culprit. Stop watering for a while to see if the spot heals.

- Should leaf tips turn brown, unbalanced watering practices are likely the cause.

JON'S INTERIOR DESIGN TIPS

Luau: This spectacular "palm" is a lovely tabletop plant when little. Use it as a centerpiece to a buffet table at a tropical theme party. Place candles around the base to highlight its interesting shape.

Contemporary: Because the shape of the ponytail palm is so beautiful and unique, it makes a great statement in a modern ultrasleek environment. It is a perfect choice for a modern office space as well.

Bonsai: Given slow growth and character, especially early in life, the ponytail palm makes a great bonsai.

RABBIT'S FOOT FERN

Davallia species

Also Known As: *Ball Fern, Deer Foot Fern,* or *Squirrel's Foot Fern*

Care: Moderate

Humidity: High

Temperature: 60 - 75°F

Fertilize: Every two weeks

Water: Lightly, often

Growth Habit: Bushy. Slow growing

Height: 12 to 18 in.

Flowers: None

All of the common names of the many varieties of this plant refer to a furry-footed animal that is brownish in color. Perhaps this is a clue to some aspect of this fern's appearance. In fact, it is. There exists on every rabbit's foot fern a structure called a rhizome. It is a root-like structure that grows laterally, under the surface of soil, or directly above it. On the bottom it sends down roots through the soil. On the top it sends up new shoots. The rabbit's foot fern has rhizomes that grow just along the surface of the soil. They are brown and have white "fur" growing over them. They feel soft to the touch and are shaped like little paws.

It is impossible to resist the urge to pet them, just once, to be sure they are not real. As the plant grows, the rhizomes will grow to the edge of the pot, and then begin to cascade over the sides.

GROWING TIPS

- Mist the rhizomes often to prevent them from drying out.

- Do not bury the rhizomes. Keep soil off the top of them.

- Water lightly, but often.

- Be careful of salt build-up near the rhizomes. Repot if necessary.

JON'S INTERIOR DESIGN TIPS

Hanging Basket: In order to see the interestingly shaped and draping "feet," a hanging basket is essential. What an interesting conversation piece this will make.

TRIVIA - The rabbit's foot fern is native to Fiji.

REX BEGONIA

Begonia rex

Also Known As: *Fancy-leaf Begonia*

Care: Moderate

Humidity: High

Temperature: 65 - 75°F

Fertilize: Every two weeks. Monthly in winter

Water: Frequently, yet lightly. Keep soil moist

Growth Habit: Bushy or trailing

Height: 12 in.

Flower: Small. Insignificant

There are many types of begonias that are often grown for their awesome flowers. There is also a large selection of hybrids that are grown for their equally outstanding foliage instead. The leaves of the rex begonia are available in nearly every color and pattern. They vary widely in shape and size, from simple ovals to complex star patterns. The colored designs on the leaves often resemble intricate mosaics. Others resemble beautifully painted watercolors. Whatever the variety, they are each unique works of art, and like snowflakes, it is certain that no two will ever be alike.

Rex begonias do bloom occasionally as interior plants, but are not grown for their blooms, which pale in comparison to their spectacular leaves. It is actually better to pinch flowers off to maintain vigor in new and existing leaves, its works of art.

GROWING TIPS

- Rex begonias appreciate the same conditions as orchids and ferns. They can be grown together.

- Rex begonias do not enjoy relocation. Pick a spot and, if it thrives, keep it there.

- Should leaves turn yellow and drop, cut back on watering.

- Should leaf color fade and the leaf become brittle, increase humidity and light.

- Never use a leaf shine product on begonia leaves.

JON'S INTERIOR DESIGN TIPS

Holiday Decorating: Try some of the varieties available for differing visual effect. The Begonia rex 'Merry Christmas', as one would expect, offers red and green colored leaves. For autumn centerpieces, try the Rex begonia 'Her Majesty' that boasts an earthy brown and cream-colored palette. It is especially nice for Thanksgiving color schemes.

TRIVIA - The rex begonia is named after Michel Begon, who was the governor of Haiti in the mid seventeenth century.

SPIDER PLANT

Chlorophytum comosum

Also Known As: *Airplane Plant*

Care: Easy

Humidity: Low

Temperature: 65 - 75°F

Fertilize: Every two weeks

Water: Allow soil to dry out between waterings

Growth Habit: Upward from a central crown, arching

Height: 10 to 12 in.

Flowers: Small, white. Flowers easily

Spider plants may well be the most recognizable of all interior plants. They can be identified by the multitude of dangling baby "spiders" that hang off the mother plant. Some refer to them as "airplanes," the offshoots dangling like little airplanes from a child's mobile over the top of a crib.

In the fall the mother plant will send up sprays of white flowers, followed by the birth of baby "spiderettes," or miniature airplanes. The babies are actually complete plants that can be snipped off and set into water to root and eventually create new plants. Or they may remain attached and they will continue to grow and eventually have babies of their own.

The leaves of the spider plant are thin, slender straps that grow from a central point in a rosette pattern. The strap-like leaves are light green and have a white stripe running down the center. They are sharply tapered at the end giving them the look of wild grass. This plant makes a wonderful hanging specimen.

GROWING TIPS

• Even though the spider plant is rather sturdy, it is very sensitive to contaminants in the water used to hydrate its roots. It is especially sensitive to fluoride in tap water. If at all possible, use distilled water.

• Should leaf color become weak and dull, increase light exposure.

• Should the plant not flower, it cannot send out "baby" plants. Therefore, make certain that the plant has complete darkness at night for approximately three weeks in the fall.

JON'S INTERIOR DESIGN TIPS

Seventies Retro: If this isn't the quintessential 1970s interior plant, I don't know what is.

Children's Room: Children love spider plants. They are not only fun, but educational as well. The replanting of the dangling babies is a rainy day project just waiting to happen.

TRIVIA - Spider plants have been grown as interior plants for 200 years.

BIRD OF PARADISE

Strelitzia reginae

Also Known As: *Crane Flower*

Care: Moderate

Humidity: High

Temperature: 60 - 80°F

Fertilize: Heavy, twice a month. Most birds of paradise are underfertilized

Water: Moderate. Let dry out between waterings. Water less in winter as sunlight diminishes. Water more in spring as sunlight increases

Growth Habit: Slow

Height: 3 to 4 ft.

Flowers: Purple, blue, and orange blooms appear on long sturdy stems. Long lasting in fall

This tropical evergreen perennial is valued for its unique bird-like orange, blue, and white blossoms. The graceful flowers that appear on long sturdy stalks resemble the feathered heads of the exotic crane or a bird of paradise, after which the plant is named. The brightly colored petals of vibrant orange that make up the crest of the bird's head are feathered and stand upright. A triple-tuft of purple petals grows separately and is angled to form the bird's forward plume. A green and pink tinted bract, at the base of the flower, is sharply pointed and appears to form the beak.

Accenting the floral artistry of the blossoms are the very large and leathery leaves of the plant. They have a blue-grey hue and are oblong in shape. It is not a coincidence that they resemble a banana leaf, as the plant is in fact related to the banana tree. When potted, the birds nesting within the thick stand of leaves creates a tropical vignette that mimics a jungle scene, much like a bonsai can imitate a forest.

Most botanists agree that the bird of paradise is named after Queen Charlotte, the wife of King George III of England, who was born in Mecklenburg - Strelitz in Germany.

GROWING TIPS

• Should leaves turn brown or blackish on the ends, the plant is too cold.

• Humidity refers to moisture in the air, not in the soil. Big difference. Keep a spray bottle nearby to mist the air around it. Do this once a day in a very dry room (every other day if humidity is average). Also mist if leaves turn brown and curl back.

• Pot bound plants promote bloom production.

• The most common reason a plant fails to bloom is that the plant is too young. Give it love and time. Blooms will appear on a plant four to five years old.

JON'S INTERIOR DESIGN TIPS

General: The bird of paradise is at home in both contemporary and traditional decors.

TRIVIA - The bird of paradise is actually considered an herb and is heavily propagated in Hawaii and Southern California.

BLUSHING PHILODENDRON

Philodendron erubescens

Also Known As: *Climbing Philodendron*

Care: Easy

Humidity: Moderate

Temperature: 65 - 85°F

Fertilize: Every two weeks during spring and summer. Monthly during fall and winter

Water: Keep soil slightly moist at all times

Growth Habit: Climbing

Height: 5 to 6 ft.

Flowers: Insignificant

The similarities between the blushing philodendron and the heart-leaf philodendron are many. Both climbing plants have heart-shaped leaves and a strong will to survive. The blushing philodendron has leaves that are more elongated. Perhaps its most brilliant feature is the bright reddish hue of new leaves as they unfurl from similarly colored new stems. Although it is a blushing beauty, it is in no way shy.

A vigorous climber, even more so then the heart-leaf variety, the blushing philodendron can be trained to attach itself to a support provided. It is a moderately fast grower that will reach 6 feet in length within a few years.

GROWING TIPS

- Repot every spring, while carefully handling the pole or trellis on which the climbing vine is attached.

- Try the 'red emerald' hybrid. New leaves and stems are red and change back to green with age.

- Should new leaves appear small and weak, the plant is in need of more nutrients. Fertilize more often.

- Should large gaps between leaves exist, provide your plant more light, as the plant is stretching to find it on its own.

JON'S INTERIOR DESIGN TIPS

General: As a young specimen, this plant makes a perfect table centerpiece. The bright reddish hue of new leaves and stems will be the topic of conversation at tonight's dinner table.

BUDDHIST PINE

Podocarpus macrophyllus

Also Known As: *Kasumaki* or *Japanese Yew*

Care: Easy

Humidity: Moderate

Temperature: 40 - 70°F

Fertilize: Monthly

Water: Keep soil moist

Growth Habit: Upright and vertical. Very slow growing

Height: 6 to 8 ft. indoors

Flowers: None

There is a single trick to growing this plant, and the key to its whole survival: it must be housed in a cool room. The Buddhist pine even enjoys cool drafts.

The Buddhist pine is not a pine tree at all, nor is it a type of yew that so many tend to believe. It is, however, a tree. The Buddhist pine you select for your interior will be a baby tree, for if you attempted to grow an adult tree you would be required to raise your home's roofline 30 feet or more. As an interior plant, the Buddhist pine can be expected to reach 6 feet if allowed to grow freely.

Leaves of the Buddhist pine look like soft pine needles that have been ironed. Their flattened appearance is similar to a yew, but they are more linear and brush-like, not lacy. They are very soft to the touch, and even though they look delicate, they are not. It can withstand low humidity and low light. It doesn't prefer these conditions, but can handle them in moderation.

GROWING TIPS

- Young specimens have a tendency to grow straight up. Continue pinching back to encourage horizontal branching instead.

- Keep cool, but no colder then 40°F.

- Mist leaves often if the temperature rises.

- Keep the plant away from fireplaces, radiators, or other heat sources.

- Make certain that the soil is impeccably drained, or you may have to deal with root rot.

JON'S INTERIOR DESIGN TIPS

General: I love this slow-growing, long-living, and very graceful plant. It is one plant that many people have for a lifetime.

Bonsai: If interested in learning about bonsai, take on your first project by using a Buddhist pine. They make extraordinary specimens.

Cottage Style: If you have a cottage that is a bit on the drafty side or a summer porch that is noninsulated and cooler in the winter, this is the plant for you, especially if you are trying to create a woodsy, lakeside or country cottage ambience.

CABBAGE TREE

Cordyline terminalis

Also Known As: *New Zealand Cabbage Palm* or *Good Luck Tree*

Care: Easy

Humidity: Moderate

Temperature: 60 - 85°F

Fertilize: Every two weeks, balanced liquid fertilizer

Water: Keep moist in growing seasons. Let soil dry out between waterings in winter

Growth Habit: Upright, fountain shaped, tree form. Slow growing

Height: 5 ft. or more

Flowers: White

You may not recognize this plant by name, but you most likely have seen it around town. It is a very popular plant in other countries, particularly Australia, Asia and the Pacific. It has a great many fans, so many that there exists an International Cordyline Society devoted solely to this wonderful plant.

The cabbage tree plant is used extensively in outdoor landscaping, but they also make a reliable and beautiful interior plant for those who live in cooler climates. In some Polynesian cultures, the cabbage tree plant is placed near the front door to bring good luck.

The leaves of the cabbage tree plant are usually red, burgundy, or pink in color and either splashed, tinged, or striated, which is part of its appeal. This is not just another solid green sword-leafed palm. It is nearly trunkless and produces its leaves in a symmetrical whorl of long strap leaves that can reach a foot or more in length. The mood set by this plant is instantly lush and tropical.

GROWING TIPS

- The cabbage tree plant is sensitive to fluoridated water. Use distilled water only.

- The plant may become deficient in magnesium. Visit your garden center to find a plant food that contains this mineral.

- Should leaf color fade or revert to solid green, the plant is not getting sufficient light.

- Should leaf tips turn brown, increase air humidity. Mist daily.

JON'S INTERIOR DESIGN TIPS

General: Cabbage tree plants are often sold as annuals and used in outdoor potted plants. The same type of arrangement can be created indoors.

Garden Basket: Grow cabbage tree plants in a mixed basket of other interior plants. Pick low growing plants and vines. For springtime displays, add forced bulbs like tulips and narcissus for a winning, late-winter display.

TRIVIA - The cabbage tree plant is high in carbohydrate content. The Maori of New Zealand used to cook and eat it.

CALAMONDIN

Citrus mitis

Also Known As: *Miniature Orange*

Care: Easy

Humidity: Moderate

Temperature: 65 - 75°F

Fertilize: Every two weeks with a balanced blend.

Water: Keep soil moist at all times during spring and summer. Let dry between waterings in fall and winter

Growth Habit: Upright, shrubby, tree

Height: 4 ft.

Flowers: White, fragrant flowers that become fruit in fall

If you have a fantasy of growing your very own orange tree, but don't live in Florida or California, then this is the plant for you. An orange tree? Indoors? Yes, it can be done. You can even eat the fruit from the calamondin. Very cool!

Fruit from the ever beautiful and fragrant calamondin is actually a cross between a kumquat and an orange. It is a bit tart and aromatic and can be used in cooking and jam making. The dark green, oval leaves are 1 to 2 inches long and have a citrus fragrance of their own. This fabulous tree grows to about 4 feet and is an exceptional interior plant to grow in a sunny South-facing window, even if you don't live in Florida.

GROWING TIPS

• When purchasing a calamondin, select one that is raised from a root cutting, not seed. This distinction is important for the plant raised from a root cutting bears superior fruit.

• The fruit from the calamondin is not big and juicy like those found at the supermarket. They are smaller and can be slightly bitter, but very aromatic and fabulous for cooking.

• The Meyer lemon, famous in the culinary world, is a miniature citrus tree that is also suitable for growing indoors.

• Keep the room humid. If blossoms drop, increase humidity.

• Should the plant not flower, either the plant container was too big or the plant was overfertilized.

JON'S INTERIOR DESIGN TIPS

Kitchen: The kitchen is an obvious place for an orange tree, especially if your kitchen is decorated in a sunny Mediterranean or Provençal theme. This plant looks stunning in a cobalt blue pot. Let the sun shine in with a calamondin.

TRIVIA - In the Philippines, juice squeezed from calamondin fruit is used to remove ink stains from fabric.

CHINESE FAN PALM

Livistona chinensis

Care: Easy

Humidity: Medium

Temperature: 60 - 80°F

Fertilize: Monthly in summer, do not feed in winter

Water: Keep soil moist. All palms must have excellent drainage. No standing water, ever

Growth Habit: Upright, jungly. Slow growing

Height: 2 to 3 ft. and taller

Flowers: Nonshowy white and cream. Rarely blooms as an interior plant

Palms, generally speaking, have two different leaf shapes, pinnate (feathery) and palmate (fan shaped). An example of pinnate is the feathery type of palm often seen in travel brochures, featuring tall trees with long silky fronds swaying in the tropical breeze. An example of a palmate palm is the Chinese fan palm.

A palmate frond is one that has three or four or more leaflets or lobes, generated from one starting point. It is just as easy to say that it is a frond that is shaped like an open palm with fingers extended. The Chinese fan palm has an added characteristic in that the ends of its fronds droop slightly downward. This armature generates a lushness and movement of the fronds.

A mature plant will grow tall enough to have a tall trunk. As an interior plant, you can expect the Chinese fan palm to keep its multiple "branches." Many people think it makes a better young specimen then a full-grown tree. And indeed it does, especially for the average home.

GROWING TIPS

- Palms are sensitive to salt build-up. Therefore make certain the soil blend selected promotes good drainage. Try mixing African violet potting mix to your soil.

- Treat your plant to a cool (not cold) shower now and then. The light spray from your shower will clean otherwise hard to clean leaves

- Should new growth produce smaller leaves, the plant needs to be fertilized. Don't overdo it.

- Should leaves turn yellow and fade, decrease light exposure or move the plant to a shadier location.

JON'S INTERIOR DESIGN TIPS

Riviera: Chinese fan palms grow in the areas surrounding the Mediterranean Sea. A French or Italian Riviera interior with sun-washed stone floors and stucco walls would provide this plant the perfect home-away-from-home.

TRIVIA - The Chinese fan palm is native to Japan and Taiwan.

CROTON VARIETIES

Codiaeum species

Also Known As: *Joseph's Coat*

Care: Moderate

Temperature: Warm

Humidity: Very High. Mist often

Fertilize: Every two weeks with liquid fertilizer. Do not feed in winters

Water: Keep soil moist. Do not allow soil to dry out

Growth Habit: Upright, bushy

Height: Up to 3 ft.

Flowers: Small, cream-colored blooms. Insignificant

The big leaves of the croton display a rainbow of colors usually reserved for flowers only. Who knew that foliage could be the life of the party? This technicolor show-stopper bears its leaves in an upright habit. It boasts stiff, heavily lobed leaves with pronounced veins of various colors. Yellow, red, orange, and green are the primary colors that become more vivid with plenty of light and age.

GROWING TIPS

Caution The leaves of crotons are poisonous. Keep out of the reach of small children.

- Keep in mind that if the room temperature rises higher then 65- 70 the chance for spider mites and aphids increases.

- Repot every one to two years.

- If new growth is undersized and sparse, increase exposure to light.

- If the leaf tips turn brown, the air might be too dry. Mist often.

- If the variegated leaves are mostly green, increase light to get brighter colors.

JON'S INTERIOR DESIGN TIPS

Tropical: Crotons will fit into any tropical home decor, as they are native to the Pacific Islands and Malaysia. They would be perfectly suited in a rainforest theme bathroom. Create a garden retreat by placing several plants around a soaking tub; or near a bright, glass shower enclosure. Crotons will love the humidity. You, in turn, will love the bright upbeat colors.

African: An African or safari inspired design would be enhanced by the geometric, colored leaves of the croton. The croton would be the perfect compliment to African textiles and masks.

Tablescapes: Try planting smaller crotons in a terrarium or under a cloche (bell jar). They will love their new tropical home, under glass. You'll be enchanted with your miniature garden and any children nearby will be able to look only, and not touch.

EARTH STAR

Cryptanthus acaulis

Also Known As: *Starfish Plant*

Care: Easy

Humidity: Moderate

Temperature: 60 - 75°F

Fertilize: Monthly

Water: Keep soil moist. Fill the "cup" every two weeks

Growth Habit: Star-shaped rosette pattern

Height: 5 to 6 in.

Flowers: Long, red bract with tiny, yellow flowers at base

The earth star is a small bromeliad epiphyte and one best for growing indoors. It rarely grows taller then 6 inches in height and looks great as a single specimen or when grown in a group with other plants. Its rosette at the center forms a flattened star shape that is exquisite. The leaves are slightly ruffled and variegated with subtle or bold stripes. Increased light will intensify the color of both the leaves and the rosette.

GROWING TIPS

• The earth star takes moisture and nutrients in through its leaves. Never use leaf polish on this plant for it will interfere with plant food and water absorption.

• If water sits too long in the "cup", rotting may occur. Remove long-standing water with a turkey-basting bulb.

• Given plant root systems are shallow, the bromeliad should be planted in a small pot.

JON'S INTERIOR DESIGN TIPS

General: The earth star is one of my favorite bromeliads. I especially like to work with the brown variegated varieties like *C. zonatus* and *C. fosterianus*. There are black variegated varieties to chose from that are equally intriguing.

Terrariums: This small bromeliad looks stunning in a miniature gardenscape. The humidity captured inside will keep this bromeliad happy and healthy.

FIDDLE-LEAF FIG

Ficus lyrata

Also Known As: *Banjo Fig*

Care: Easy

Humidity: Moderate

Temperature: 60 - 85°F

Fertilize: Monthly. Keep soil moist at all times

Growth Habit: Tall, multibranching or single-stemmed. Slow growing

Height: 8 ft. indoors or taller. Up to 30 ft. outdoors

Flowers: Seldom flowers indoors

There is no way to say this gently. This guy is a monster, an exceptionally benign, big green giant. And he is about as lovable as can be. The leaves are huge and friendly looking. They are rounded and lobed, and shaped like fiddles. At over a foot in length, the leaves of the fiddle-leaf fig are hard to ignore.

One can select a specimen that has multiple branches that will grow lush and bushy, or select one with a single trunk (often braided) to allow it to grow into a standard size tree. Either way, the overall impact is powerful and impossible to ignore.

GROWING TIPS

• This plant is big. Make certain that you have enough elbowroom for it to grow. It is best to keep it in one place as it resents relocation.

• Prune early during the plant's development to encourage branching.

• Plant in a heavy pot to prevent the heavy leaves from toppling the plant over.

• Keep the big leaves of this striking plant clean with a damp, soft cloth.

JON'S INTERIOR DESIGN TIPS

General: Unable to purchase a piece of artwork for a large, empty wall? Introduce the fiddle-leaf fig with unique leaf and growth pattern – Mother Nature's works of art. Up-light for nighttime drama.

TRIVIA - In the rainforest, the fiddle-leaf fig begins as an epiphyte to eventually become a tree, living on its own.

FISHTAIL PALM

Caryota mitis

Also Known As: *Burmese Fishtail Palm* or *Clustered Fishtail Palm*

Care: Easy

Humidity: Moderate - High

Temperature: 65 - 85°F

Fertilize: Monthly

Water: Let soil dry out slightly between waterings. Never let soil get "bone dry"

Growth Habit: Upright clump, palm-shaped

Height: 3 to 5 ft. indoors. Up to 25 ft. in native habitat

Flowers: Not indoors

The fishtail-shaped leaves of the fishtail palm are its distinguishing feature. The leaves are comprised of two triangular segments that are frayed on the ends, much like a fishtail. The bipinnate leaves look as if they have been deliberately cut into the shape of a mermaid tail. The overall sheen to each leaf is silvery, thus adding to the whole fishtail motif. As an interior plant it is likely to grow to 3 to 5 feet at the most.

GROWING TIPS

- Use large deep pots when plants are younger. As the plant ages, allow the roots to become pot bound.

- Mist daily in heated air of winter.

- Given available space, move the plant outdoors during the summer.

- Should leaves on the bottom of the plant turn brown, this is natural. Simply cut them off. Never tear them off.

- As with all palms, never prune unless a branch dies or becomes broken.

JON'S INTERIOR DESIGN TIPS

Tropical: Use as you would any palm-shaped interior plant.

Entertainment Rooms: This plant is perfect for any game room filled with large aquariums or fishing trophies. Move this plant outdoors in the summer to add a bit of whimsy to your pool house.

TRIVIA - The fishtail palm will grow 6 to 8 inches per year.

HEDGEHOG CACTUS

Echinocereus pectinatus

Care: Easy

Humidity: Low

Temperature: 65 - 80°F

Fertilize: Monthly, with a high phosphorous blend, to encourage flowering

Water: Let soil dry out completely. Water lightly

Growth Habit: Slow growing

Height: Varies widely

Flowers: All cacti flower. Common colors are red, pink, and yellow. On mature plants only

Many people write off the "lowly" cactus as the cartoon-like hedgehog of the botanical world. Cacti are highly evolved, flowering perennials that over the eons shed their leaves in favor of spines and opted to store water for survival in their rounded, fat bodies.

Most of us associate cactus with deserts only. But cactus can be found in alpine regions of Europe. There are two basic types of cactus: desert and forest types. Desert cactus include those commonly seen in your favorite cowboy movies. They generally are spiny with a globe or elongated shape. This description well describes one of my favorites, the hedgehog cactus. Forest types have flatter leaf shapes that tend to trail. This group includes the popular season favorite, the Christmas cactus (see chapter 6: Celebrate the Seasons).

The following information is generally true of all cacti. Should you chose to experiment with an unusual variety of cacti, use the following information as general guidelines:

GROWING TIPS

Caution Teach your children to respect the cacti's spines.

- Overwatering of cacti during winter months is the most common cause of plant death.

- Cacti need a soil mix that drains quickly. Look for soils in your home improvement store made especially for cacti.

- Plant cactus in clay pots for improved drainage.

- Should any part of the plant turn black, the plant is likely being overwatered.

- Should the cactus begin to shrivel, it is in need of water. It will recover quickly.

- Should the cactus fail to bloom, the cactus is either too young or in need of additional hours of light.

JON'S INTERIOR DESIGN TIPS

Dish Gardens / Children's Gardens: Children are naturally curious about cacti. The incredible variety of plant shapes and bright colors of their flowers are fascinating. These are perfect plants to use in a tabletop garden.

INDOOR BAMBOO

Poganatherum panaceum

Also Known As: *Bamboo*

Care: Easy

Humidity: Moderate to High

Temperature: 50 - 75°F

Fertilize: Monthly

Water: Keep moist. Will thrive while sitting in water

Growth Habit: Bushy

Height: 5 to 6 in.

Flowers: None

Growing bamboo as an interior plant is increasing in popularity. Once considered only an Eastern plant, the Western world has embraced bamboo for its delicate leaves, rapid growth, and instant Zen-like ambience.

There are many types of bamboo from which to choose. Many look-a-likes are labeled as such in local nurseries, but are not actually true bamboo. Which varieties of bamboo are suitable for growing indoors? My particular favorite is the indoor bamboo that will grow with roots entirely submerged in water, making a sort of "ecosystem" and an interesting conversation piece.

Phyllostachys nigra is a large bamboo that can be grown in large tubs if you have the space and the light source required. Dwarf types such as *Arundinaria* are much better suited for indoor living.

GROWING TIPS

- Keep in cooler locations and away from heat sources.

- Bamboos can be successfully grown indoors if provided adequate light and humid conditions. The bathroom counter or windowsill is likely the perfect place to start.

- Should leaves drop suddenly, increase light levels. New leaves more tolerant of new light conditions will grow to replace the old leaves.

- Make certain soil has excellent drainage.

- Bamboo needs air circulation. Place in entryways or near drafty windows.

JON'S INTERIOR DESIGN TIPS

Oriental Chic: In an Asian-inspired interior, you cannot miss with the introduction of indoor bamboo. Slip your waterproof container into a wooden Chinese rice bowl to make a more authentic arrangement. A nearby light will cast a beautiful silhouette of this plant to create nighttime drama.

TRIVIA - Indoor bamboo is native to Malaysia.

LACY LEAF SELLOUM

Philodendrun bipinnatifidum

Also Known As: *Anchor Philodendron*

Care: Easy

Humidity: High, but will tolerate moderate humidity

Temperature: 60 - 80°F

Fertilize: Monthly

Water: Let soil dry out slightly between waterings

Growth Habit: Upright in youth. Bushy and spreading with maturity

Height: 6 to 8 ft. tall indoors

Flowers: Insignificant

We associate vining and trailing plant characteristics to the philodendron. The lacy leaf selloum is one of the rarities of this group. It produces a central stem that is strong and upright. Its leaves are truly stunners. In mature plants, leaves can reach 3 feet in length. They are deeply scalloped and grow on long, thick stalks. When the plant is young, it is more upright in habit, but as it ages it relaxes and allows its stalks to lean outward, giving it a bushier appearance. As it matures further, it will become much wider than it is taller.

One of the exceptional features of this plant is its habit of sending out aerial roots at the base. They are sometimes referred to as anchor roots. It is all right to cut them off or tuck them into the pot, or even to let them hang down over the side of the container, which adds an unconventional twist to your display.

GROWING TIPS

- Lacy leaf selloums are big plants and require plenty of room.

- Repot every one to two years.

- Lacy leaf selloums like humidity, but will survive on moderate air moisture. Be indulgent and give it a misting now and then. It will reward you for your kindness.

- Provide a support as the plant grows larger.

JON'S INTERIOR DESIGN TIPS

Industrial/Modern: Philodendrons are attractive in most types of interiors, provided they are given enough bright light. The largest philodendrons should perhaps be reserved for rooms with tall ceilings and expansive glass doors and windows commonly found in the contemporary home.

Floor Specimen: A large philodendron, either climbing or nonclimbing, can make a wonderful focal point for a large room. If you have a smaller plant, place it on a pedestal or a planter with legs to increase its height. Its large splashy leaves will take center stage.

MISTLETOE FIG

Ficus diversifolia

Also Known As: *Mistletoe Rubber Plant*

Care: Easy

Humidity: Moderate

Temperature: 60 - 75°F, but will tolerate higher temperatures

Fertilize: Monthly

Water: Keep soil lightly moist

Growth Habit: Bushy, jungly. Slow growing

Height: 3 ft.

Flowers: Small white and green fruits. Prolific

The mistletoe fig is an easy-to-care-for ficus that is ideal for the indoor gardener. The foliage is outstanding and made even more interesting by the zigzagging branches that hold fan-shaped leaves. This is one of the few ficus species to develop fruit indoors. The yellow or white fruits are abundant and have a pronounced presence. The species can eventually achieve a height of 3 to 5 feet. It likes humidity and high temperatures, but is not tolerant of droughts or overwatering.

GROWING TIPS

- This is one of the easiest ficus to maintain.

- Keep soil moist, but not boggy.

- Let the berries grow. There is no need to cut them off for the sake of the foliage.

JON'S INTERIOR DESIGN TIPS

Holiday Décor: It would be unfortunate if the mistletoe fig was not utilized in your holiday decorating. Place plants amongst candles and centerpieces. Use individual plants as hostess gifts by setting one at each place setting, tied with ribbon and a name card. The mistletoe fig can even take the heat when placed near the fireplace. Just be sure to water and mist often.

PEPEROMIA

Peperomia species

Also Known As: *Watermelon Begonia*

Care: Moderate

Humidity: Medium, but will tolerate less

Temperature: 65 - 75°F

Fertilize: Twice a month

Water: Allow soil to dry out between waterings

Growth Habit: Trailing, bushy or upright

Height: 6 to 10 in. for trailing plants, 4 to 6 in. for bushy plants, 12 in. for upright plants

Flowers: Tiny white blooms on tall thin stalks

There are at least a thousand species of peperomia. Who knew such a cute little interior plant had so many kinfolk. And like families, they may have different leaves, but they all seem to like the same things, which is mainly bright light, average room temperature, and lightly moist soil.

With so many species available, it is easy to find a peperomia that is just right for your needs. There are trailing, upright, and bushy varieties. They are available in varying lengths and heights, but they will all stay compact and small. Most peperomia are semisucculent in nature, therefore their leaves and stems are thick and fleshy and hold water.

The peperomia is easy to identify by the marking on its leaves resembling those of a watermelon. It is as if someone painted a 3-D version of the melon right onto the leaves. It is horticultural tomfoolery at its finest and a lighthearted addition to any interior space.

GROWING TIPS

- Repot every spring.

- Should leaves die suddenly, it is most likely due to burning from overfertilizing. Cut off the damaged leaves and repot with fresh soil.

- Overwatering is the most frequent cause of death.

- Keep in bright indirect light, but know that less light is acceptable.

JON'S INTERIOR DESIGN TIPS

Dish Gardens: Because of its compact size and interesting foliage, peperomia are perfect for dish gardens. Peperomia can be a bit tricky in terrariums because it is easy for them to rot from too much soil moisture.

Office Gifts: This plant is a great gift for coworkers because of its interesting appearance and manageable size.

Indoor Picnic: Rained out? Brighten everyone's spirit with a picnic indoors. Decorate your table with peperomia to bring a touch of the outdoors in. See who is first to notice this plant's resemblance to the watermelon for dessert.

POLKA DOT PLANT

Hypoestes phyllostachya

Also Known As: *Freckle Face*

Care: Easy

Humidity: Medium to High

Temperature: 65 - 80°F

Fertilize: Every two weeks during growing season

Water: Keep soil moist

Growth Habit: Open and bushy, fast growing, not long living

Height: 12 in.

Flowers: Small spikes of purple flowers, occasionally on interior plants. Best to cut them off as they deplete vigor from the plant

The polka dot plant is grown for its colorful, patterned, oval leaves. It features a fresh pink and white color with splashes of dark rose against a background of green. The pretty shades of pink set this plant apart in a world of verdant green interior plants. While it is a diminutive plant when grown in a dish garden, it can reach a foot tall when grown alone as a specimen.

Recently, the polka dot plant is being used as a bedding plant outdoors. It makes for a beautiful addition to a garden border. Like other interior plants, it can be moved outdoors in the summer and brought indoors given the threat of frost. Do not wait until it is too late.

GROWING TIPS

- Without sufficient light, patterned leaves will return to solid green.

- Never place in direct sun, as the leaves will scorch. Although a high-light plant, it needs a bit of protection.

- Repot if plant gets potbound.

- Prune back hard if the plant gets too leggy.

- The brighter the light, the less scraggly the stems will become.

JON'S INTERIOR DESIGN TIPS

Dish Gardens/Terrariums: Use as you would the nerve plant to showcase eye-catching foliage in a tiny garden setting.

TRIVIA - Polka dot plants are native to Madagascar.

RUBBER TREE PLANT

Ficus elastica

Also Known As: *Indian Rubber Tree*

Care: Easy

Humidity: Medium

Temperature: 50 - 80°F

Fertilize: Every two weeks

Water: Weekly, when top of soil is dry

Growth Habit: Upright

Height: 8 to 10 ft.

Flowers: Seldom flowers indoors

The rubber tree plant is one of the most popular interior plants of all time. This is most likely due to its bold and dramatic silhouette, and reputation as an easy-to-care-for plant. Leaves grow to a foot in length and 6 inches in width. They are deep green, thick and sturdy, and have an extraordinary gloss on the surface, one that rivals the factory finish on a new car. The underside of the leaf is brown in color and feels soft to the touch, quite like brushed leather in texture.

The rubber tree plant has a central stem that just keeps growing, taller and taller. It is reminiscent of the plant in the cartoon versions of Jack and the Beanstalk. This native to India and Malaysia is known to grow to 120 feet or more in height when grown in its native habitat. As an interior plant, one can expect it to grow 8 to 10 feet or until it reaches the ceiling. At this point your main task will be in keeping the extraordinary leaves free of dust.

When shopping for plants, be sure to select one that is free of any markings on the foliage. Obviously, you do not want to bring plant diseases or insects home with you. But also remember that marks or tiny tears on the leaves will form scars that will remain for the entire life of the plant.

GROWING TIPS

- Rubber tree plants grow best when the roots are pot bound.
- Dust leaves with a damp cloth regularly to prevent spider mites.

JON'S INTERIOR DESIGN TIPS

Retro: How many old black and white TV shows can you remember that showcased the rubber tree plant as decoration in the room? There are many. Use a rubber plant in your home to create a vintage 1950s mood.

Victorian: Every parlor in Victorian England had a rubber tree plant in the corner. Try recreating this look with a magnificent pot on an ebony plant stand.

TRIVIA - The sap from the rubber tree plant was used to make rubber, until the Pará rubber tree took over the task.

SCHEFFLERA

Schefflera actinophylla

Also Known As: *Octopus Plant* or *Umbrella Tree*

Care: Easy

Temperature: 65 - 80°F

Humidity: Moderate

Fertilize: Monthly

Water: Allow top 1 inch of soil to dry out between waterings

Growth Habit: Vertical, treelike, longlived

Height: 7 to 8 ft.

Flowers: Attractive long flowers, rarely blooms indoors

The leaves of the schefflera are its most distinctive feature. They are compound leaves with individual, elongated leaflets that grow in a circular pattern, creating a pinwheel effect. They are shiny and vivid green and grow on long thin stems. Younger leaves have fewer leaflets, usually four to six. As the plant grows taller, the number of leaflets will increase to twelve to fourteen in number.

You can grow this plant as a bushy shrub by pinching it back, or allow it to grow taller into a tree-like shape by just leaving it be. Since scheffleras are easy to take care of and relatively inexpensive, they are the perfect plant to take home, especially if you are a beginner. Nothing could be a cheerier addition to your home than the schefflera with its bright green silhouette and, of course, its jaunty little umbrellas.

GROWING TIPS

- Grow in a heavy pot to prevent the plant from toppling over.

- Keep leaves clean to keep spider mites away.

- To keep the plant erect, stake the main stalk as the plant grows. Should this not be done, it is likely to grow crooked as it twists and turns to get maximum light exposure.

- Mist regularly.

- It is common for lower leaves to drop as the plant gets taller.

JON'S INTERIOR DESIGN TIPS

Contemporary: The shape of schefflera leaf clusters and the height of this plant make it a perfect "sculpture" to soften the hard edges of a sleek, contemporary interior. Place an up light on the floor below the plant to cast shadows of the leaves on the ceiling and wall behind it.

TRIVIA - The schefflera plant is named after an explorer in South America who rode across the continent on horseback.

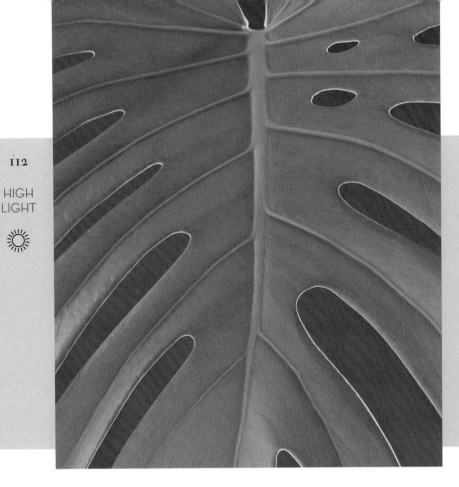

SWISS CHEESE PLANT

Monstera deliciosa

Also Known As: *Monstera* or *Split-leaf Philodendron*

Care: Easy

Humidity: Moderate

Temperature: 65 - 85°F

Fertilize: Monthly

Water: Allow soil to dry out between waterings

Growth Habit: Climber with aerial roots

Height: 6 to 8 ft.

Flowers: Rarely flowers indoors

Leaves with holes in them? Why on earth would you want a plant with such leaves? Well, if the leaves are big, heart-shaped, and shiny, and the pattern of holes appear as though skillfully cut by design reminiscent of paper snowflakes, you might change your disposition. Unique, beautiful leaf designs are in fact exactly why the Swiss cheese plant is sought after.

This is a sturdy plant with a strong presence. A talented climber with aerial roots that will attach to a moss pole easily, the Swiss cheese plant will quickly establish a root system and begin its vigorous climb, up to 8 feet tall. As the plant grows, leaves will become larger and more deeply notched. In its native habitat, a single leaf can reach 2 feet across. Should you keep the plant staked and growing vertically, scalloped leaf patterns will become even more pronounced.

GROWING TIPS

- Repot every year.
- Train to grow up a vertical moss pole or trellis.
- Keep away from drafts.
- Keep leaves free of dust.
- Should leaves remain small and lack scalloped holes, the plant is likely receiving too much light.
- Should leaf tips turn brown, water more frequently.

JON'S INTERIOR DESIGN TIPS

General: This is a dramatic floor plant. Keep it in a large, heavy pot to prevent a nasty spill. Consider using a pot with simple design and form, to keep it from competing visually with the interesting leaves of this plant.

Passageways/Room Dividers: In a large doorway or great room with two separate functional areas, place a plant on both sides of the doorway or along the wall on the imaginary line that divides the two areas. Created is an archway that will help greet guests, as well direct traffic with style.

TRIVIA - Although nicknamed the split-leaf philodendron, the Swiss cheese plant is not a philodendron.

WEEPING FIG

Ficus benjamina

Also Known As: *Fig Tree* or *Ficus Tree*

Care: Moderate

Humidity: Moderate

Temperature: 65 - 75°F

Fertilize: Monthly

Water: Allow top 2 inches of soil to dry out between waterings

Growth Habit: Bushy, weeping branches, easily trained into a tree. Slow growing

Height: 7 to 9 ft.

Flowers: Rarely

If all of the interior designers in the world had to create a small interior tree that would add exemplary beauty, texture, and mood to an interior space, they would probably come up with a plant much like the weeping fig. The delicate canopy of dainty oval leaves that grow atop an upright silver grey trunk is as graceful as one can imagine for an interior plant. The weeping habit of the branches contributes to its beauty.

When you go to the nursery to purchase a weeping fig, look for one in a pot that appears too small. Weeping figs are commonly available with a braided trunk, a feature that becomes more pronounced with age. The ornamental trunk can introduce a bit of sophistication to your home.

GROWING TIPS

- Weeping figs do not tolerate ongoing relocation. Keep in one place.

- It is common for 20 percent of the leaves to fall off each year, usually in late winter.

- Should the tree appear top heavy (given the small pot selected to promote a healthy plant), place the pot inside a heavier pot to maintain plant stability.

- Since branches are weepy, this plant is easy to accidentally overwater. Yellowing leaves are the best sign of overwatering.

JON'S INTERIOR DESIGN TIPS

Romantic: When placed near a sheer-covered window, the weeping fig adds a decidedly romantic airiness to any room.

Cottage: Bring the forest inside, to accent the painted country cottage look you have embraced.

Mediterranean: The leaves of the weeping fig are similar to a laurel tree, or bay tree, that grow in Italy and the Mediterranean region. Place your fig in a clay pot and dish, directly onto the tiled floor in your family room or kitchen. Hang dried herbs or pots of rosemary in a window nearby. Viola! Your efforts will take you to a sunny warm place, even in the depths of winter.

TRADITIONAL HOMES
& TRADITIONAL PLANTS

Reach beyond your comfort zone.

Most baby-boomers grew up in what is considered a "traditional" home, located in one of many subdivisions. It was common to find these medium-sized homes cut into more rooms than needed. Often found in these homes were a front foyer, living room and dining room (used only for Thanksgiving and other holiday meals), a big family room, a kitchen connected to a two-car garage, two to four bedrooms, several bathrooms, and a few crazy family members.

Given the number of rooms, most were small. Unless the home had vaulted ceilings (increasingly popular in the early 1980s), there truly wasn't enough room to accommodate larger plants, especially after the introduction of oversized furniture, kids, and the family pets.

My old two-story farmhouse in Pennsylvania is traditional but far smaller than what I have described. From the middle of the family room, I can water plants, talk on the phone, prepare dinner, feed the dogs, and pay bills – all at the same time (no big surprise if you know me at all). Because of its low, 8-foot ceilings, I usually decorate at home with smaller plants.

Despite the lack of wiggle room in most traditional homes, especially mine, it's important that we realize we do not have to settle for only **AFRICAN VIOLET**–sized plants. If you're inventive, you will find ways to introduce some larger interior plants so you can enjoy their beautiful appearance and personalities as well. Tall orchids are commonly found in my bathrooms. The medium-sized **PEACE LILY** and even larger **ZZ PLANT** are placed on the floor of my two bedrooms upstairs.

A large and beautiful **SCHEFFLERA** is placed in front of the French doors on the back wall of my combined office/family/dining room. It serves me well as a privacy screen, spoiling any plots the occasional peeping Tom might have.

My dangling 6-foot **HEART-LEAF PHILODENDRON** – I call this the "reach-out-and-touch-someone" plant – has a permanent place on a shelf directly above the entrance to my walk-in shower. Here it grows to its little heart-leaf's content. This touch of whimsy makes showering fun for weekend guests. This plant reminds me of the many grapevine swings my brother Dusty and I clung to while swinging over the Rockcastle River. Don't tell Momma.

When selecting plants for your next home project, get your feet wet by picking a room in your home that is not used on a daily basis. Your dining room and guest bedroom are likely candidates. Place a large plant that is perhaps out-of-scale on the center of the dining room table or atop a sidetable in the bedroom, or even in the bathroom. You may find that you like the look.

As I write this, a large **SPATHIPHYLLUM** potted in an antique, silver champagne bucket serves as my dinning room table centerpiece. Without fail, it is the topic of predinner conversation. Is it a practical location for my small table for six? No. But the few times a month I do host dinner parties, I simply relocate it to a more practical but temporary spot, just before dinner is served.

In this chapter you'll discover more out-of-the box plant ideas for small- to medium-sized traditional homes.

Plants that prefer high humidity are often happiest near sinks or bathroom showers. Keep the cook company with a cool *maidenhair fern*.

This cozy corner is complete with the *fiddle leaf fig* (far left) and *mistletoe fig* (near left). This space has vivid floral photos, floral pillows, and a cutflower arrangement, so it is not in need of plants with additional flowers. All-green plants will bring dimension and life to this corner without competing with the décor.

A soft, luxurious room with oversized couch, chairs and pillows calls for the soft, oversized oval leaves of the *birds of paradise* (left and right). This pair towers over the corners of this couch to give guests a bit more privacy from other conversations taking place outdoors, without having to draw heavy drapery. The *snakeskin fern* (center) provides a bit more life to this formal room.

With its light-green leaves and wandering curly tendrils, low-light *grape ivy* is used to brighten dark corners.

All types of *bonsai* plants add an air of sophistication. Unfortunately its small root system requires a dedicated watering schedule, making it less than ideal for someone who travels often.

If you have never slept on a screened-in porch, you are missing out on one of the greatest pleasures of life. The large *schefflera* (right) atop the antique trunk sitting at the foot of this iron bed and the *trumpet vine* crawling up the outside of the sunniest side of this porch provide all the shade and privacy needed for a midday nap. *English ivy* topped with a touch of *African violets* (left) rests on the nightstand.

Two oversized *rhapis palms* make a bold statement on this bathroom dresser.

The *heart-leaf philodendron* (top center) was hung above this shower door to produce a jungle-like feeling. The water-loving *indoor bamboo* (middle and bottom) couldn't be happier in this moist retreat.

This rustic room with stained wood French doors and windows, wood cabinets and beams, and cold stone floor begs for a splash of warmth. The maroon and green colors from the center rug were the inspirations for the pair of forest green *schefflera* plants (left wall). They make a wonderful first impression paired with the antique 1940s bar-cloth throw pillows with maroon fringe. The tropical leaf pattern of the pillows and the table centerpiece of cut maroon flowers extends the tropical theme introduced by this pair.

Short on wall space? The retired blue toolbox (floor) overflowing with *fittonia* comes in handy again as a planter. Cut hydrangea branches resting in the sink behind will be beautiful in tonight's floral centerpiece.

This *spathiphyllum* (center), formerly my dining room table centerpiece, finds a temporary home on my family room coffee table during dinner. For brunch the next morning, it remains out of the way to hide a quiet fireplace. Medium-light *Cobra ferns* (left and right) are suitable for the corners of these bookcases and are given some light from side windows and doors.

Afternoon delight!
The reds in the
kalanchoe (left) and
rubber plant (right)
pick up the warm
colors in the rug and
throw pillows.

A beautiful bathroom is a home's sanctuary, a place to start and end the day. *Indoor bamboo* (left) thrives best in the wettest conditions. What better place to put this plant than in the bathroom with a steamy shower. With its upright variegated leaf, the *dieffenbachia* (right) in a galvanized trough fills the void between the bathroom mirror and the vanity. *Heart-leaf philodendron* vine (above) adds the finishing touches.

This furniture collection with its many sharp edges needs a bit of softening to make it a bit more inviting. The soft and pliable leaves of the *euphorbia* (top right) and *spider plant* (bottom left) do just that.

The kitchen table is my favorite place for collections of plants. They can be enjoyed during every meal and every time I walk by the table. Sweet smelling *jasmine* will be the topic of conversation at tonight's dinner table. Surprise your family with a different plant now and then.

My garden shed is a wonderful place to store large plants such as this *parlor palm* for the winter, provided the temperature doesn't fall below 55°F. A space heater can give you some peace of mind while you're transitioning plants from warm weather to cool and back again.

From this kitchen stool, a child can get a first hand look at the new twins in town. Never mind the neighbors: I'm talking about the pair of *snake skin ferns* Momma just brought home from the annual plant swap. Participation in these events are a good way to learn about indoor plants.

CONTEMPORARY HOMES & CONTEMPORARY PLANTS

Even the most modern space can be transformed.

Beginning in the 1970s, the promise of less-expensive office and manufacturing parks in the suburbs drew many companies, along with their employees, out from the heart of many American cities. In time, downtown offices, manufacturing buildings, and homes were left empty.

Beginning in the 1990s, however, cities experienced a rebirth of these neighborhoods, drawing lost inhabitants and their families back to downtown areas to again call the city their home. For many, suburban life did not provide them with the endless sources of excitement and convenience of a big city. Many inhabitants were also happy to leave suburban traffic congestion and homogenization behind.

Given a new demand for housing, deserted buildings were converted to residential loft spaces. Sleek, open, contemporary interior designs – popular with younger generations – best suited these spaces because of their tall ceilings and oversized windows. These large-scale features, while providing plenty of interior room and natural sunlight perfect for the introduction of larger interior plants (some to grow as big as trees), also introduced new interior design problems. Lack of privacy and warmth topped the list.

Even in suburbs today, older homes are finding a new life after cosmetic changes transform their dated interiors into more contemporary, open-construction living spaces. These larger rooms need dramatic interior plant shapes and life to "command" the room.

In this chapter, you'll discover many interior plant solutions for a contemporary space. Still not convinced of their design benefits? Look at these photographs of selected spaces to see a dramatic improvement in the appearance and warmth of these rooms. What added benefits could these ideas bring to your own contemporary living space?

Plants of any stature might make this dinning room table with high-back chairs a bit claustrophobic. And why compete with the extraordinary artwork hung at this table's far end? Use low-lying *baby's tears* in several containers to introduce a subtle breath of fresh air.

"Art imitates life." Or is it "Life imitates art"? Either way, what a smashing combination this Richard Anuszkiewicz painting and *calathea* make.

This large and colorful Robert Goodnough abstract painting is the focal point of this room. Instead of competing, the *bromeliad* with its purple headdress complements this piece.

A hidden windowsill is now a planter for *dracaena 'lemon-lime'*, giving life to a lonely corner of this contemporary kitchen.

By placing a tree-shaped, *striped dracaena* inside, an immediate connection to the outdoor trees is made, inviting the outside in. The aluminum container reflects the contemporary feel of the room.

My favorite palm, the *fishtail palm*, is perfect for this empty but sunlit family room corner. The simple, soft, clean lines of this furniture and accessories need a plant with a bit of contrasting edge. The height of this palm connects this room's high ceilings with sunken furniture while its bare stalks allow for a view of outdoor rooftop underplantings.

A sleek, wooden countertop made with shapely curves is adorned perfectly here with a bowl of *African violets*. One of the most common plants is made extraordinarily chic in this setting.

These three *succulents* are each unique in shape and color, but all are attractive when placed together in look-alike pots. This collection was added to the small coffee table to enhance the rustic, outdoor feeling of the furniture.

BEFORE & AFTER

Plants really do change a room. Even in the most stylish modern designs, or in a luxurious traditional home, the right plant can make a memorable addition. Take a look at how adding the right living accessory makes these rooms come alive.

BEFORE: This contemporary breakfast room of cool colors is beautifully appointed with stainless steel stools, a polished marble-top table, stylish, low-back chairs, and mohair and silk pillows. A large stainless steel window separates the seating nook from the beautiful garden planted atop this home's rooftop.

AFTER: Invite the outdoors in! *Mother-in-law's tongues* with firm, wavy, upright tendrils appear to move and blur the line between indoors and out. Three plants are huddled together on one side to provide a portion of the seating area with a bit more privacy. A watermelon with similar color and variegation makes for a temporary but creative coffee table centerpiece.

BEFORE: The tall bedroom window of this downtown city apartment overlooks unappealing city construction but provides this otherwise dark corner with light and warmth.

AFTER: Let the sunshine in. The dimensions of this *pencil cactus* are perfect to cover the window. Its upright and unique pencil-shaped foliage commands your full attention while allowing full sun to pass. The worries of the outside world are gone. (Art by Robert Goodnough.)

CELEBRATE THE SEASONS

In the same way that **CROCUSES** are the harbingers of spring, the **POINSETTIA** heralds in the holiday season. We associate the **CHRYSANTHEMUM** with fall, the **TULIP** with Easter, the **ROSE** with summer. We traditionally form strong connections with these symbols of the seasons. The cycles of nature's year unfolds in a predictable order that becomes a comforting pattern in our lives. We know what is to come each year, yet it is the anticipation of the beauties and mysteries of each season that we value.

As the **DAFFODILS** push up through the earth to unfold their jaunty blooms, we can see ourselves as a child picking one from the neighbor's garden to give to our mother. As we gaze out the window at the golden shower of leaves from an oak tree, we remember Halloweens of years gone by. The connections are immediate and powerful.

Each season gives us a reason to gather with others, either in celebration or simply to enjoy the company of friends. Why not draw loved ones to the table with unique living centerpieces? They spark conversation year-round and can be combined easily with colorful specialty plants specifically chosen for the season.

In this chapter I hope to inspire you to use seasonal specialty plants and living centerpieces to mark the changing year.

Living Centerpieces

There is certainly something to be said about living in sunny climes where the weather is always warm and predictable. But, if you grew up in areas of our country such as my current home in Pennsylvania, there was always the excitement of the first snow, the fresh smells of spring, the heavy night air of summer and the crisp air of fall. I know that for me the changing seasons are required in my life just as much as plants and dogs.

Since Mother Nature takes care of all of the interesting changes on the outside of my home, for the inside I bring in seasonal plants to keep the feeling going. I pick up small

CELEBRATE SUMMER with a cool breeze and beautiful terrariums. A collection of various sizes and shapes are gathered here at lunchtime for an unforgettable centerpiece. Despite the use of different plants, repetition of a single color makes for a coordinated setting. Glass containers allow visitors a sneak peak of how each was constructed.

HONOR SPRING with a display of seedlings started in anticipation of warmer weather. Even the coldest morning will be warmed by this sign of good things to come.

pots of flowering plants that are available in each season and insert them into a larger, longer-lasting planting. These are then used as the center-piece of the kitchen or dining room table, or on the coffee table in the living room. The "longer-lasting" plants are easy care greens that look good on their own, but are perked up with the addition of a **PAPER-WHITE** in the winter or a colorful **KALANCHOE** in the summer. Using large shallow dishes with gravel for drainage, I can plant ivies, ferns, or succulents and create a terrific conversation piece.

These living centerpieces are a pleasure to look at daily and are an inexpensive alternative to cut flowers. Give them some pizzazz with lichens, mosses, stones, marbles, and of course, seasonal plants.

The living branches of *coleus* rooted in unusual and varied glass containers add beauty and color to an otherwise bare table.

This arrangement of *birds nest fern* (back), *selaginella* (front), and *hens and chicks* (right) – with a bird nest/robin's eggs centerpiece – is perfectly appointed to welcome spring. Avoid disaster at the Easter table by using imitation nests and eggs. These little blue soaps were returned to Momma's bathroom once brunch was over. *Note: I don't recommend stealing nests from their feathered tenants. This nest was inadvertently hauled away with a shrub.*

Christmas cactus celebrates this holiday in its own unique way. Look fast – its blooms won't last but are a joy to behold.

Seasonal Specialty Plants

For most interior and exterior plants, I apply the following motto: *Find plants that have the shape and leaves you like, for this is what you are going to live with most of the year. If it flowers, that is a bonus.* But with a very select group of plants – seasonal specialty plants – the flowers are their gift to us. The seasonal specialty plant has traditionally been selected, not for its foliage, but for the beauty of its fragrant and colorful flowers. The word *seasonal* is the operative word to remember, however. The flower of each variety blooms only once each year (seasonally) coinciding with the coming of a new season or celebration of a religious holiday.

With the exception of the **CHRISTMAS CACTUS,** I recommend these be discarded after they are finished blooming. They do not rebloom under ordinary house conditions. If you wish to attempt a rebloom, then hooray for you. But don't feel guilty about trashing them – along with the Easter eggs well past their prime or the uneaten holiday fruit cake – to make room for your favorites associated with the next season. By practicing this approach, you will enjoy flowering plants at their very best, year round, and you will prevent the stockpiling of past beauty queens.

Below is a list of a few of my favorite seasonal specialty plants. Those in bold receive special emphasis with descriptive profiles on the pages to follow.

Spring:
PANSY, azalea, crocus, daffodil, Easter lily, hyacinth, hydrangea, primrose, and tulip

Summer:
KALANCHOE, Asiatic and oriental lily, caladium, campanula, flowering begonia, fuschia, and geranium

Fall:
CHRYSANTHEMUMS, cyclamen, florist gloxinia, geranium, nertera, ornamental pepper, pin cushion flower, penta, and slipper flower

Winter:
CHRISTMAS CACTUS, amaryllis, cinerarias, coleus, heather, paper-white, and poinsettia

PANSY

Viola x wittrockiana

Care: Easy

Humidity: Moderate

Temperature: 60 - 70°F, but will tolerate temperatures as low as 40°F

Fertilize: Monthly

Water: Keep soil slightly moist at all times. Do not overwater

Height: Up to 8 in.

Flowers: Purples, yellows, and white. Large

Often we associate the pansy with outdoor planting and quick spring color for our beds and borders. While pansies are indeed lovely additions to the gardens outside of our homes, they also make sassy little indoor plants as well. Pansies have the ability to brighten up any spring soiree, from fancy to humble. Either way, they will be at home. The intensely hued flowers have large, flat-faced petals with bright brush strokes of often contrasting color. They are reminiscent of a painter's palette that is swirled with pigments from the artist's brush. There are generally five petals to each of the long-lasting flowers.

GROWING TIPS

• Pansies like cooler growing conditions. Keep away from heat sources including radiators and fireplaces.

• Deadhead old blossoms to encourage new blooms.

• Make sure they get plenty of sunlight.

JON'S INTERIOR DESIGN TIPS

General: The blooms of pansies are very tasty. Yes, you can eat them. They are a creative addition to salads.

Spring Forward: Welcome in the spring. Place several pansies in a ceramic bowl with a blanket of sheet moss to use as a table centerpiece. Add faux bird's nest and robin's eggs, or equally colorful Easter eggs to the mix to surprise your Sunday guests.

TRIVIA - Pansies are related to violets.

KALANCHOE

Kalanchoe blossfeldiana

Also known as: *Flaming Kathy*

Care: Easy

Humidity: Low

Temperature: 70 – 90°F, but keep cooler in winter

Fertilize: Every two weeks while flowering

Water: Allow soil to dry out between waterings

Growth Habit: Low growing with leaves in a rosette pattern

Height: 4 to 8 in.

Flowers: Small, brightly colored flowers in clusters

The kalanchoe is a one of the happiest little plants you'll ever come across. It is easy to care for and is very generous. It will cheerfully share with you its abundant blooms, in a veritable rainbow of summer colors: red, orange, pink, and yellow. Each individual flower is tiny. But they are massed together in a single panicle that itself is lilliputian, like miniature dollhouse bouquets. The effect is lovely and endearing. Take it a step further and mass several plants together in one basket for an even more stunning effect.

The kalanchoe is a succulent. Its leaves are thick and fleshy and hold water. Therefore it can withstand periods of dryness, much like a cactus. It is an ideal addition to a home that is warm with plenty of bright light.

You will likely find kalanchoe in nearly any large supermarket or garden center. Often you'll see them smiling at you from the garden department shelves. Go ahead and smile back. You've made a new friend. And a delightful friend at that.

GROWING TIPS

- Kalanchoe will tolerate dry air and warm temperatures.
- Let plants rest after blooms are through by watering less and providing less light. This will encourage blooming later in the year.

JON'S INTERIOR DESIGN TIPS

Cottage Style: Kalanchoe is beautiful with a casual country feel all their own. It is well suited for the relaxed style of a cottage home. It would look beautiful atop a piece of English painted furniture. Imagine a single plant on a cupboard near a kitchen window with white linen curtains. Should your kitchen be warm with activity, all the better for your new addition.

TRIVIA - Kalanchoe is native to the island of Madagascar.

CHRYSANTHEMUM

Dendranthema grandiflora

Care: Easy

Humidity: Low

Temperature: 60 - 70°F

Fertilize: None

Water: Let soil dry out slightly between watering

Growth Habit: Upright, bushy

Height: 6 to 12 in.

Flowers: Yellow, maroon, white, orange, rust, ruby, yellow

The Chrysanthemum Throne refers to the Japanese monarchy, which is considered to be the oldest continuing monarchy in the world. The chrysanthemum plant itself has an equally long history as it has been in domestication for well over 2000 years. Its reputation as a reliable and beautiful flowing plant hasn't wavered much over the centuries. In modern times, science has brought many improvements and hybrids. The "mum" is most likely going to remain one of our most popular flowering plants for centuries to come.

Flower heads of the mum are most often dahlia shaped. Should you think mums are played out, look for varieties with unusual blooms, like those shaped like stars, buttons, spiders, and daisies. Most mums have a pleasant, earthy fragrance that to many of us brings back memories of high school homecomings, Halloween parties or sunny fall days. It is difficult to imagine this time of year without the regal, emotive chrysanthemum somewhere in the picture.

GROWING TIPS

- Should you purchase mums after they have produced buds or blooms, you will not need to fertilize them.

- Should lower leaves become soft and gray, the plant may have a fungal infection. Move the plant to a warmer location and allow soil to dry out between waterings.

- Should leaves turn yellow, the humidity may be too high. Move the plant to a drier location.

JON'S INTERIOR DESIGN TIPS

General: Mums can be divided loosely into two categories: florist mums and garden (or hardy) mums. Florist mums are cultivated for indoor growing.

TRIVIA - The National Chrysanthemum Society claims that mums were first grown in China over 2000 years ago.

CHRISTMAS CACTUS

Schlumbergera truncata

Also known as: *Holiday Cactus*

Care: Easy

Humidity: Medium

Temperature: 65 - 80°F in summer; 50 - 65°F in winter

Fertilize: Every two weeks with a high phosphorous blend

Water: Keep moist in heat of summer. Water less in winter

Growth Habit: Open, with arching segmented branches

Height: 8 to 12 in.

Flowers: Multi-tiered petals dangle from stems. Flowers are red, pink, or orange

A Christmas cactus in full bloom is a site to behold. It boasts red, orange, pink, or white blossoms on the end of glossy, flat succulent segments. Stems grow in a long, bowing sweep that hang over the side of the container. The shape of this plant resembles a giant crab with its segmented legs and sprawling outward growth. Their flowers resemble those of orchids in their beauty and complexity. In fact, the Christmas cactus is an epiphyte, just like an orchid. This means that, in nature, it is found growing while hanging on the branches of trees, in the canopy of the rainforest. Its roots cling to the branches of the tree from which it receives its nutrients and water.

Remember its natural habitat when caring for a Christmas cactus indoors. It is essential that the cactus receive bright light, air movement, and adequate amounts of water.

GROWING TIPS

- We typically think of cacti as being heat-tolerant, but Christmas cacti will keep their blossoms longer in cooler temperatures.

- Keep this plant in a well-lit location away from drafts from fireplaces and other heat sources.

- Should flower buds drop from the plant prior to blooming, the plant is likely too close to a high heat source.

- Try not to handle plants once they begin to bloom, or the blooms may drop off.

JON'S INTERIOR DESIGN TIPS

General: The Christmas cactus makes an ideal plant for a pedestal or for a hanging pot.

TRIVIA - The Christmas cactus is pollinated by hummingbirds in native forests.

IT'S A FAMILY AFFAIR

I will be forever thankful for my childhood.

My childhood was spent on our verdant piece of Kentucky property nestled along the Rockcastle River and surrounded by the Daniel Boone National Forest. Ironically, it was the things we did without (such as televisions or phones) that drove me and my brothers and sisters outdoors to explore our property.

The outdoors became our primary source of entertainment. There was always something to excite us on the next hill and or just beyond the next tree. Some days were spent swinging from grapevines into the Rockcastle River, fishing for bluegills and sun grannies, picking teaberry leaves, or occasionally laying quietly in the beds of moss and lichens that covered the forest floor. Others were spent learning to avoid the stinging nettles. There were caves to explore, canoeing adventures, and animals to care for – including dogs, cats, peacocks, guineas, mules, and horses. Who had time to watch television anyway? The outdoors was our teacher. Through our adventures, we acquired a valuable respect for Mother Nature and her beauty, strength, and vulnerability.

Unfortunately today, many children – especially those living in cities and suburbs – spend hours on end indoors, being entertained with television, videos, and computer games. Without an introduction to the outdoors, they remain unaware of the far more interesting adventures and lifetime memories that await them.

Here are several ideas for introducing or reacquainting the children in your home to the wonders of the outdoors. The adult children might learn something too.

Ecosystems

1. Using a waterproof container a minimum of 3 inches tall, create your own ecosystem using water-loving interior plants such as indoor **BAMBOO** or **PAPYRUS**. Think old crockery for a traditional look, or a clear glass dish for a more contemporary look.

2. Add gravel, polished stones, or marbles around the plant's root system to provide your plant firm support.

3. Top the whole thing off with a turtle or two. Very cool.

The kitchen is the heart of the home. I like to find a place, either on the counter, center of the table, or sideboard to display my "living centerpieces." From the *papyrus plant* (below), Egyptians made the first writing paper. This beautiful plant will make the perfect kitchen counter centerpiece and topic of conversation as hungry guests and family members anticipate the upcoming meal. And it won't hurt that the kids will think they have the hippest parents in town.

Aquariums

Build an aquarium without all the fixin's (tank, sunken ship, pirates, and seaweed). Try this easier, more unique, and far less expensive approach:

1. Find a clear heart-shaped container like the one pictured here. Carefully add stone, gravel, or marbles to the bottom of your container. Fill roughly 80 percent with distilled water and a family of goldfish.

2. Carefully remove the dirt from the roots of any water-loving plant. For the cleanest results, you may consider rinsing the roots in a separate container of distilled water.

3. Next, carefully submerge the roots into your container until their top is completely immersed in water. Should the water line in the container not rise within a half-inch of the neck of this container, add additional water.

4. Using sticks from the yard, fashion a cross that will rest on top of the neck of the container to provide a support for your plant.

Jump on in, the water is just fine. . . at least this family of four thinks so as they explore their new watering hole. Goldfish will need a filter – especially with a narrow-necked vase such as this – whereas Bettas (Siamese fighting fish) don't require a filter, and they will love swimming among the roots of a *peace lily*.

Terrariums

For me, terrariums bring back memories of the '70s – big hair, bell-bottoms, cool cars, and second grade science experiments. From my terrarium (a pickle jar), I was fascinated to see grass seed grow green and tall in rich soil atop a layer of stone. Consistent watering and proper light conditions, I learned, were the key to my success. This experience sparked my interest in horticulture, and later a rewarding career in gardening.

Look around! What's old is new again. The '70s are back. Some big hairstyles are once again in vogue. Bell-bottom pants you swore you would never again wear now hang in your closet. Get even hipper by introducing terrariums to your children.

If you're feeling adventurous, try building a terrarium in a jar with a narrow mouth. Don't worry, this is easy compared to building model ships inside bottles. It takes some getting used to, but you'll get the hang of it. Here's how:

1. First locate an over-sized jar. A jar with a narrow opening will best mimic a greenhouse environment. My beautiful old jar was found in a local antique store.

2. Using a large-mouth funnel (shown is one fashioned from a broken miniature clay pot), pour in gravel for drainage, then level. Two to three inches of gravel will be sufficient for drainage.

3. Add 2 to 3 inches of a lightweight soil mixture. Spread evenly across the surface of the gravel. You're ready for the fun part – planting.

4. Select plants that are moisture loving, pliable, and easily divided such as *fittonia,* mosses, and ferns. Each plant should be of equal light tolerance. Carefully subdivide each plant into smaller portions that can easily navigate the narrow jar opening without plant damage. One by one, drop each plant portion into the opening of the jar.

5. Using tape and/or twine, fasten a small, narrow spoon (baby spoon or relish spoon) to the end of a thin but sturdy straight stick or dowel (long enough to reach the bottom of your jar) to create your own tool for planting. You will use this tool to create holes for your plants and maneuver them into place. Use the spoon to cover any exposed roots with excess dirt.

6. Drop in decorative stones if you wish. Lightly water. For this particular terrarium, we started with a cup of water. Remember, the moist atmosphere in the bottle will demand for far less watering than the potted houseplant.

Viola! No one needs to know how easy it was. Kids will love keeping your secret.

What a conversation piece! Without the lid to this wide-mouth terrarium, plants are permitted to grow beyond the container. However, moisture will be lost, therefore calling for additional hand watering. This terrarium, filled with *succulents* and lichens and mosses found in the woods behind my house, will grow best in the sunniest locations.

Seed Starting

Get a jump-start on your spring gardening season. Beginning indoors in early spring, I start plants from seed in beautiful, glass containers that line the windowsills of my home's kitchen and potting shed.

Lettuces and many herbs are easy to germinate indoors. Despite my many years of seedstarting, the indoor germination process remains a special experience to observe during early morning coffee and evening meals. The slow and steady growth of a plant from seed in the comfort of your own home is relaxing; the thrill of experiencing spring indoors and well before the threat of frost is exhilarating.

Seeds with hard outer shells like those of **MOONFLOWER** and **MORNING GLORY** vines are notoriously difficult to start outdoors. Get better results by starting them indoors.

Seeds harvested from last year's vines can be soaked overnight in water and planted in containers along a sunny windowsill (see photo at right). From each seed, seedlings of 2 to 3 inches will grow and (after the threat of frost is over) will be transplanted along the foot of my garden fence and corner posts of my front porch to connect my home to the earth.

Get a jump-start on spring. This galvanized tray accommodates nine seedlings.

To promote interest early on, involve your children in the seed selection process. Your local hardware and home-improvement stores will fascinate them with hundreds of vegetable and flower seeds from which to choose. The directions are easy to follow and are included on each seed packet.

Lettuce and herbs are easily started in this collection of classic glass urns. A bell jar helps to provide this lettuce seedling with the perfect growing conditions.

This windowsill provides a nice sunny location for starting seeds in early spring. *Moonflower* seeds are soaking overnight to break open the hard seed shell.

Plant Rooting

Many interior and exterior plants, even some trees, can be started from parent plant clippings simply by dropping a fresh clipping in water. Once roots are established, clippings from exterior plants are planted outdoors in garden borders or containers to grow to maturity. Clippings from indoor plants are potted and often given away as gifts. This method requires very little materials and even less time and effort.

To establish long roots (at least 6 inches in length), I recommend that clippings be taken from parent plants no shorter than 1 foot in length. From the 6 inches (or more) of stem sacrificed for root growth, leaves should be removed prior to rooting. Allow roots to grow 1 to 2 inches long. The longer the roots, the better chance the plant has for survival.

From the 6-foot, *heart-leaf philodendron* hanging above the opening to my walk-in shower, I often clip smaller vines to promote a healthier parent plant. Once firmly rooted, the prize clipping is given away to a previous plant admirer.

For containers, I prefer tall (2 to 3 feet), glass cylinders. The height of these containers will protect weaker clippings from bending and breaking, and keep taller and sturdier ones from leaning – eventually toppling the root container over. Glass is recommended to maximize the clipping's exposure to light, allowing development of strong roots below the water's surface.

For lighter-weight clippings (vines, soft branch), I recommend the cylinder used be filled only halfway to discourage the clipping from floating and falling out of the cylinder. For heavier clippings (hard branch), you can fill it up.

I traditionally begin rooting plants in early spring of each year. Cylinders filled with clippings are often huddled together on coffee tables to create unique and interesting centerpieces.

From the **COLEUS** plants I've overwintered in my potting shed each year, I take dozens of clippings and root them. Eventually they are planted in the borders of my garden and in containers on the back patio. The 15-foot curly willow tree behind my house began as a successful rooting. A dozen more clippings are taken from this single tree each year to f ulfill client and family orders.

Functional and beautiful, the *curly willow, heart-leaf philodendron*, and *Swedish ivy* are all easy to root in water.

Introduce big kids to plants. Even the busiest workspaces have room for a plant to connect people with the earth in the midst of hectic demands. The upright foliage of the miniature *spathiphyllum* (above) and the *anthurium* (right) do not crowd either workspace. The roots of the anturium cling to lava rock resting in a simple stone tray of water. There's no guesswork as to when to water this arrangement. Simply keep the stone container filled.

An exotic plant like the *cobra fern* (left) with its snake like characteristics can capture the curiosity of even a young boy. Awesome!

Whether just outside the bedroom door, on the windowsill above a bathroom sink, or in the kitchen where family meals are cooked and the events of the day are discussed, greet your family each day with plants. With smaller plants, try multiples for more "wow" factor. This collections of *haworthias* fits comfortably along the available narrow windowsills.

Tired of getting Dad Westerns or underwear for his birthday? This *snakeskin fern* with reptile-like skin matches the masculine theme of this bamboo tray, and silver and snake-wrapped magnifying glasses.

No room on the windowsill? This three-tiered caddy makes the most effective use of limited space in a small kitchen.

No need to put your shoes on for a trek to the garden. This windowsill provides the happy cook the perfect sunlight to grow herbs at his/her fingertips. Fresh tomatoes kept in a glass bell jar, *basil* (left), and *thyme* (right) await mozzarella and olive oil.

Papyrus

PAPYRUS is an ancient plant that is strongly associated with the Egyptians, though sadly now it is almost gone from its natural habitat along the Nile River. Today it is cultivated in plantations and is available as an ornamental plant. The grass-like leaves were commonly used as an Egyptian design element. Nearly every part of the plant was utilized in some form to enhance the life of the Egyptians. Parts of the plant were eaten or made into fuel, while the stem was used in ancient Egypt to make mats, cloth, sails, sandals, and most well-known, paper.

Although it is not impossible to grow the larger *Cyperus papyrus* indoors, there are dwarf varieties that are easier to grow and maintain indoors. Try *Cyperus haspan*, which is sometimes referred to as the pygmy papyrus, paper reed, or umbrella plant; or the *Cyprus diffusus* that is called the dwarf papyrus. Papyrus is easy to maintain as an interior plant if you follow some basic rules.

DESIGN TIPS: Students, bring this plant to school for show-and-tell. This plant will likely become your teacher's favorite and sit proudly on his or her desk. A few brownie points never hurt.

The World of Insectivores

The **PITCHER PLANT** and the **VENUS FLYTRAP** fall into a special category that is truly fascinating. They are called insectivores, and as the name suggests they eat insects. They do this not because they want to gross anyone out but because they must to survive. As the plants evolved through time, they acquired the ability to trap insects and to digest them for an additional source of nutrition. It is believed that these plants were growing in situations where their root systems were incapable of gathering enough nutrients from their environment. It is an amazing example of how plants have survived and evolved over the centuries.

While carnivorous plants offer a fascinating study in the evolutionary progress of life, the varying types of traps that these plants use to attract and kill their prey is equally as interesting. Active steel traps, mousetraps, flypaper traps – these are the mechanisms used by the Venus flytrap. Passive traps are employed by pitcher plants. They include pitfall traps, flypaper traps, and lobster-pot traps.

Generally the favorite prey of carnivorous plants are ants, butterflies, bees, dragonflies, flies, grasshoppers, mosquitoes, and spiders. But they will eat virtually anything that falls, climbs, or is baited into their traps. Myth and folklore surround these carnivorous plants. They are reported to be a plant that was referred to as the man-eating plant of Madagascar. However, none of this has proven to be true, so we will not add "man" to the official list of carnivorous prey. Not yet anyway.

PITCHER PLANT: All pitcher plants employ a passive pitfall trap to capture their prey. There are several wonderful and exotic varieties from which to choose. They have been know to consume small rodents and lizards that unfortunately visited the wrong address. The pitcher is composed of leaves that are folded around themselves. They look like papers loosely scrolled. The upper surface of the pitcher is smooth and covered with tiny hairs that grow downward into the pitcher. An insect is forced to slide down into the trap. Each type of pitcher plant has a slightly different pitcher formation, but the mechanism for trapping is basically the same.

DESIGN TIPS: Surprise your boys with the pitcher plant; it's cool enough to pass their discriminating tastes. Your tomboys might like them too.

Pitcher Plant

VENUS FLYTRAP: Charles Darwin has called the Venus flytrap "the most extraordinary plant in the world." That is high praise coming from the father of evolutionary studies.

The mechanism the Venus flytrap uses to catch its prey is referred to as an active steel trap. It sounds frightening, and if you are a fly, it most certainly is. Tiny hairs on the inside of its leaf trigger the trap. The trap is a double tap that prevents the leaf from closing in on something that is has accidentally caught, like a leaf or general plant debris that it does not wish to eat. However, if it does, the trap will open after twenty-four hours.

DESIGN TIPS: Pizza, sodas, chips, and a few flies comin' right up. Keep the party cool and interesting for the whole gang, including the Venus flytrap your husband will love.

Venus Flytrap

PLANT PREPARATION & CARE

Contents:

COMMON PLANTING TECHNIQUES

There are three techniques for planting your interior plant in a container. I refer to these techniques as the Plant and See, Drop and Hide, and Cachepot techniques.

Plant and See

For your plant, select a container with a drainage hole bored from the bottom. Be sure to select one deep enough to accommodate the combined depth of the plant rootball, a layer of drainage if used, and 1/2 to 1 inch of extra space to avoid overflow during watering. For added drainage (recommended for water-intolerant CACTUS and other succulents), pour stone or gravel 1/5 the depth of the container selected.

When removing your plant from its original plastic container, be sure to protect its root ball from crumbling. Drop your plant down into the center of its new container. Should the surface of your plant not stand tall enough, remove your plant and add additional, quality soil and try again. Add soil to fill voids between the rootball and the container. As with outdoor plants, it is important not to add new soil above the level that the plant was growing in its original pot.

Now the bad news: to prevent water damage, a water- and moisture-proof tray should be placed under your plant's container to catch possible water run-off. Made of porous material, the common clay saucer is not the correct choice. Clear plastic trays are perhaps the best choice for protection and appearance.

Drop and Hide

For some, a mismatching protective tray is out of the question. There is a solution. For your plant, select a container. A cachepot (a container without a drainage hole) is preferred since there is less risk of water damage. Select a container deep enough to accommodate the combined depth of the plant (in its original plant container) and its protective tray, and wide enough to accommodate the wider of the two.

Along with the protective tray, drop your plant, in its original container, inside the new container. Decorative mosses, pinecones, stones, and marbles are often placed on top of the soil surface to hide the plant's original container.

Avoid plant "wet feet" and death by carefully controlling the amount of water you provide. Should the container you selected have a drainage hole, be equally careful not to water outside the lip of the original plant container inside.

Cachepot Technique

For your plant, select a cachepot that is 1 1/2 to 2 inches deeper and a bit wider than your plant's original plastic container. Be sure to select one made of water- and moisture-proof material in order to protect the surfaces of your furniture, counters, and flooring.

Put an inch of stones or gravel at the bottom of the cachepot to prevent the roots from getting "wet feet." Drop your plant, in its original container, inside. Try the decorative ideas offered in the "Drop and Hide" technique to hide the plant's original container.

Try water-loving indoor bamboo your first time around should you have the jitters about the cachepot technique.

THE GREATEST CHALLENGE FOR THE BEST REWARD

With most endeavors in life that are worthwhile (related to school, work, home, marriage, friends, and family), the easiest part of the equation is getting started. Once the honeymoon is over, it's the keeping-it-going part – maintenance – that presents the greatest challenge.

To graduate from school, to climb the corporate ladder, to create a wonderful home environment for your family, to cultivate long-lasting friendships – to do all of these things well takes hard work, dedication, and consistent performance. Proper plant care, while fortunately far less demanding in terms of time and effort, requires this same consistency in performance.

In school, you must attend school every day and study to ensure good grades. Cramming the night before for the finals of a class you have never attended will most likely prove to be a futile exercise. Similarly, pouring gallons of water on a bone-dry plant will not cure what ails the plant if it has been neglected and left dry of water over an extended period of time.

With this in mind, establish a schedule for plant care that is consistent and enjoyable from week to week. For me, caring for my plants while enjoying my morning coffee is both relaxing and, given a second cup, energizing!

CARE BASICS

Watering

"How much water should I give my plant?" This is the number one question people ask when they either receive or purchase a plant. Since overwatering is the number one reason most plants die, perhaps the safest bet is to water only when the plant asks for it – when the plant droops. This method is, however, stressful to the plant and often a day late.

A plant's watering schedule can require adjustment because of changes in humidity, temperature, growth cycle, or even changes in the construction of a plant's container (for example from glazed to unglazed pottery). Perhaps plants would be better off if we stayed at home a bit more. In fact, watering techniques offered by my old plant care books must have assumed we all worked at home. I don't know about you, but I am not missing dinner or a night on the town to entertain plants.

How to Water

WATER PLANTS ON A REGULARLY SCHEDULED DAY OF THE WEEK.
Before each watering, use the tips of your fingers to test the soil. If dry to the touch, it is time to water. If moist, wait. After a few days, retest and water if dry.

BE AWARE THAT EVERY PLANT HAS ITS OWN WATERING NEEDS.
My **ALOE** hardly needs any water, while my **IVIES** seem to gulp the water. I leave lots of water in the drainage trays of my ivies to keep them wet and happy.

LEARN TO READ PLANT SYMPTOMS.
With a single glance, you know
when a co-worker is in poor spirits
or when a pet isn't feeling well.
Similarly, plants look different
when they are thirsty (leaves may
be slightly wilted and their color a
bit dull) than they do when satis-
fied with life-giving water.

**ALLOW TIME FOR TAP WATER TO SIT
IN A CLEAN CONTAINER OVERNIGHT.**
This will allow time for chlorine
in the water time to evaporate. Tap
water kills a store-bought goldfish
within minutes – imagine what it
will do to your plant.

SOME GENERAL RULES:
• Water more when the temperature is warm, less when cool.
• Water more when humidity is
low, less when high.
• Water plants with long narrow
leaves more, water less with succulent leaves.
• Water more in high light, less in
low light.

How to Water When You're Away

Deserve a bit of time away? If so, you should not have to worry about the welfare of
your plants while you're gone or the possibility of returning to the unthinkable. On
occasion, I've entrusted the care of my green loved ones to my "waterer" without favor-
able results. Did these plants have to scream out before getting watered? Try these more
reliable alternatives.

SINK, WATER, AND TOWEL TRICK:
Transfer your plants from their "showy" pots back into the plastic ones in which they came home. Add several inches of water in a plugged kitchen or utility sink. Dip one end of a thick, absorbent towel in the bottom of the sink while laying the rest of the towel on the (waterproof) counter or dish drain area. Place your plant, still potted in the plastic pot, on top of the towel. Viola! The towel acts as a wick to draw the water from the sink to the plant's roots as long as the water lasts. Easy, yes?

BAGGING:
Put a clear garbage or sandwich bag over your plant, taping the edges to the pot. You've created a mini greenhouse. Place sticks inside to prevent the bag from touching the plant.

WATER JARS WITH WICKS:
Place a large jar filled with water on the edge of your kitchen counter sink. Run a fabric wick (available at local hardware stores) from inside the jar to your plant resting on the bottom of the sink. Through capillary action, the wick will draw water from the jar to drip-feed your plant positioned at the other end.

Fertilizing

Each time you water your plant, water leaches nutrients from the soil to wash them away through your pots drainage. That, combined with the uptake of minerals through the plant's root system to its top growth, quickly depletes nutrients from the soil. For healthy plant growth, these nutrients must be replaced on a regular basis. Common feeding methods include foliar, time-release, and water-soluble.

FOLIAR:
This spray method is a good quick-fix for the plant that appears on its last leg. The spray is absorbed through the plant's leaves to give it the quick kick in its pants

it desperately needs until either of the other slower, but more reliable, methods (time-release or water-soluble) are able to process nutrients through the plant's root system.

TIME-RELEASE:
Fertilizer sticks, spikes, granules, and crystals provide a slow-release of nutrients. Time-release pellets are the easiest way to fertilize. These little beads are commonly found at the base of the temporary container that your plant was brought home in from the nursery. These pellets will slowly dissolve over a six- to nine-month period, feeding the plant slowly. I have found this method works best for me. I avoid overfertilization or "burning" of plants, and save time by not mixing powders, granules, or crystals. Time-release fertilizers may deliver nutrients inconsistently.

WATER-SOLUBLE:
Plants with lots of foliage require water-soluble feeding that gives the nutrients quicker access to the root systems of these plants. Most of us grew up with this popular choice. I always mix it at half the strength recommended, which rarely ever "burns" the plant. This liquid form is fast-acting and is easily measured.

MANURE TEA:
For the organic person, pick up a bag of dehydrated cow manure at your local garden supply center. Fortunately, the dehydration takes most of the odor and "burn" away. Put about a cup of the manure in an empty gallon jug and fill with water to create a "tea." This "manure tea" provides a nice food for indoor plants. It is also commercially available.

Using Fertilizers

Fertilizers are plant food. They are nutrients that your houseplants need to grow. In the same way that we need protein, carbohydrates, fats, and minerals to maintain growth, a plant has specific requirements as well. The main requirements that we need to concern ourselves with are nitrogen, phosphorous, and potassium. Other requirements include micronutrients like iron, magnesium, copper, and calcium. These nutrients can be found in chemical fertilizers that are man-made formulas, or they can be found from organic sources. Both of these types of fertilizers can be found at your local nursery or home improvement center.

Ingredients

When reading a fertilizer label, the three key ingredients are the most important. Each of these elements serves to benefit different functions in the plant's growth.

NITROGEN:
Think of the foliage when you see this. Nitrogen is responsible for leaf and stem growth. Young plants need plenty of nitrogen as they send up shoots and leaves. Nitrogen will green up your plants and help maintain foliage.

PHOSPHOROUS:
This is for flowers. When a plant is in bloom it requires a large amount of phosphorous to keep the blossoms healthy and to promote bud growth.

POTASSIUM:
This promotes root growth. The potassium in fertilizer will help to promote root growth and will also assist with the absorption of water and nutrients.

Numbers

The numbers that you see on the fertilizer package represent the ratio of one element to the next. It is always in the same order: nitrogen, phosphorous, and potassium. For example 7–7–7 indicates that the fertilizer has a balance of all three chemicals. If the numbers are 10–7–7 then the formula has more nitrogen. If the number is 7-14-7 then this fertilizer will promote blooms and healthy flowers because it contains more phosphorous.

Specialty Blends

A trip to the garden section can be confusing. The trick is to know what it is you're looking for. There are many choices with formulas perfectly blended for your particular houseplants' needs. Here are a few different types of blends:

AFRICAN VIOLET:
This blend will have a high ratio of phosphorous to promote bloom growth.

CACTI AND SUCCULENTS:
This blend is specifically formulated with the correct levels of nitrogen to maintain healthy leaves.

BLOOM PROMOTERS:
These have a high phosphorous content.

ORCHIDS:
Different ratio blends are available in this category.

Organic Fertilizer Amendments

GREEN SAND:
Contains potassium and the micro-nutrient iron; derived from marine products

BLOODMEAL:
Steamed then dried by-product of the meat industry with a high phosphorous content

FISH EMULSION:
Very mild; excellent choice for sensitive plants; smells like fish for a short while

SUPER-PHOSPHATE:
A rock phosphate that is combined with sulfuric acid to produce phosphorus (in a form easy for plants to utilize and take up from the soil)

Pruning

Plants are living things, and with all things living should come the expectation of growth and the need for periodic maintenance, particularly indoors given the confines of walls, ceilings, and floors.

On many a morning, I have dreamt of rolling straight from my bed directly to my car and work, bypassing the mundane regime of the morning shower-shave-brush. I suspect after a week of this, small children and the elderly would not dare approach. However I couldn't stand the thought of my dogs barking at me or a pinch from Momma on the back of my arm. Fortunately for everyone, my dream was short-lived.

Folks, if you want to look your best, you have to put in the time. The same goes for interior plants. Listed below are two methods of plant pruning.

Deadheading

Once a plant's blooms begin to fade, pinch them off down to the next growth node. This directs the plant's energy toward the growth of fresh foliage rather than toward the remaining seedpod.

Pinching

Long, stringy plant growth can be removed to improve plant shape by pinching off (with your fingers) unwanted portions of the growing stem back to the closest nodes. This encourages lateral shoot growth and a bushier, healthier plant. Vines such as **PHILODEN-DRONS** and **IVY** also benefit from the removal of these "straight ends."

For plants with variegated leaves, remove the occasional solid green leaf to prevent these plants from reverting to their former, nonvariegated variety.

INDOOR PLANTS LOVE HUMIDITY

My father wanted to raise his family on an island of sorts. To fulfill his dream, Daddy built our home on property nestled along the banks of Kentucky's Rockcastle River and surrounded by the Appalachian Mountains. This combination of river and moisture-retaining mountains results in year-round picturesque mornings of heavy (as high as 90 percent) fog, perfect conditions for supporting lush flora and fauna.

Many interior plants originate from jungle-like areas of the world with high, humid conditions not unlike those experienced on our property during early morning. Sixty percent humidity is required by most interior plants. Even desert cacti require humidity, at least forty percent to survive.

Unfortunately, our homes' heating and cooling systems rob needed moisture from the air. It dries our skin, causing it to wrinkle. Similarly, it produces harsh interior climates for our plants. To raise the humidity in your home, you have several options. They are listed below in the order of effectiveness.

HUMIDIFIER:
The humidifier is my favorite solution. Other than needing the periodic water refill, it is practically self-sufficient. It keeps on working while you're bringing home the bacon. Put them in rooms that have the greatest number of plants. Purchase an indoor humidity thermometer to determine if the number and placement of your humidifiers are providing adequate humidity to your plants. The target humidity level is 60 percent.

WATER MISTER:
The water mister is a good choice for providing needed moisture only if you work from home or if you don't travel extensively. Spray moisture-loving plants daily as part of your morning coffee and plant-care ritual, if it makes you happy. But once a week as part of the watering process will do the trick.

WATERPROOF SAUCER WITH STONES AND WATER:
Evaporation of water from the saucer will provide potted plants with a slow but steady source of needed moisture. Stones are added to the saucer to prevent plant roots from getting "wet feet." Don't forget to fill the tray up as needed.

COMMON PESTS

Plant pests are like unannounced visitors who turn into rude houseguests. They are uninvited, park their belongings wherever they please, keep their rooms messy, eat all the good food, invite their friends to join them, and basically take over the place. And then to make matters worse, they won't leave. You might be able to get a few of their friends to depart, but somehow they just keep coming back. How on earth did you get into this mess? Maybe you need to go back and examine how all of this happened. Did you leave the door open just a crack? How did they know you were so vulnerable?

Here is a key to recognizing common pests and protecting your plants from harm. Arm yourself with this information so that you are ready when the unwanted guests appear at your front door.

Aphids

Aphids are also known as greenflies. They are found throughout North America. There are more then 1300 species, and they can feast upon nearly any kind of plant.

SIGNS - clear, sticky secretion on leaves; growth irregularities on new leaves; distorted leaves, buds, or flowers.

CRITTER PROFILE - look for aphids on the bottom of leaves or on new leaves and buds; color: greenish yellow, pink, light brown, or black; pear-shaped bodies; always found in colonies (there is never just one or two); may have wings.

PREVENTION - keep plants healthy; inspect plants regularly for signs of infestation.

ORGANIC CONTROL METHOD - 1) rinse leaves with a firm stream of water to knock off aphids; 2) cut off damaged leaves and buds; 3) spray with insecticidal soap.

Mealybugs

Most often you will find mealybugs in the southern United States, but they are also found up North, mainly when they are propagated in greenhouses.

SIGNS - yellowed and withered leaves; white cottony patches on new growth; sticky secretion on leaves or stems.

CRITTER PROFILE - pinkish specks covered with white "fur"; pine-nut shaped bodies 1/10 of an inch in size; look for them at the leaf base (next to the stem); check soil for signs also, as some species attack roots; check the bottom of the pot also.

PREVENTION - check all new plants thoroughly for infestation; mealybugs often piggy-back on other plants; check all plants regularly; keep a particular eye on succulents, cactus, and African violets.

ORGANIC CONTROL METHOD - 1) dab a cotton swab in rubbing alcohol and swab it onto bugs to kill them, or use vegetable oil to loosen them; 2) wash off the diseased plant with a shower of soapy water; if the leaves are too sensitive, just use water and dab dry with a cloth.

Scale

This is one of the most interesting of all the houseplant invaders, albeit one of the most annoying. In their youth, scale are mobile. They crawl up the plant, and once they find a place they like, they sit down, dig in, form a hard shell to protect themselves, and never leave.

SIGNS - bumps along the stem or leaves; plant is losing vigor; new growth is weak, yellow, or distorted; sticky substance on leaves, stems, or even the tabletop near the plant.

CRITTER PROFILE - hard, waxy "shells" on undersides of leaves or on stems; look for them near the center vein; color: brown, gray, or white; flattened disk shapes with raised centers.

PREVENTION - check new houseplants carefully for infestation; keep a close eye on ficus and ferns, as they are particularly susceptible.

ORGANIC CONTROL METHOD -) cut off leaves that are damaged or heavily infested; 2) spray with insecticidal soap to loosen scales; you may need to use vegetable oil; 3) mechanically remove them with fingernail or tweezers; be careful not to damage the stems; 4) be sure to remove any scale that fall into the plant container; 5) wash the plant and treat scars with alcohol.

Spider Mites

Also called red spider mites, spider mites are tiny – so tiny that you cannot see them with the naked eye. These spiders are in fact related to ticks, but not to worry, they are not interested in humans or pets. They are strictly vegans.

Signs - leaves have tiny yellow specks (pin-prick-size) and appear stressed and weak; later stages: rusty appearance to leaves; white "webby" material on leaves (very severe infestation).

Critter Profile - microscopic eight-legged spiders; reddish brown or green in color

Prevention - maintain higher humidity because spider mites like dry conditions; give plants a regular shower; carefully check all new plants added to your collection for infestation; use magnifying glass to examine leaves.

Organic Control Method - 1) cut off severely damaged leaves and stems; 2) rinse the plant with tepid water to remove mites, or immerse it in a bucket of water; 3) spray with insecticidal soap or pyrethrin.

Whiteflies

In Florida, California, the Gulf states, and the West, whiteflies live outdoors. In other areas of the country, whiteflies live in greenhouses. This is often how they make their way into your home, hitching a ride on your new purchase. Inspecting all plants thoroughly before you adopt them goes a long way in preventing a whitefly infestation.

Signs - loss of plant vigor; small swarm of flies rise up when plant is watered or disturbed; whitish green lice-shaped larvae on leaves, usually on the underside; whiteflies congregate on the tops of the leaves.

Critter Profile - tiny flies with white wings; adults are 1 millimeter long.

Prevention - keep plants on a regular watering schedule; monitor all new plants coming into your house; be particularly alert to patio plants that are coming inside for the winter.

Organic Control Method - 1) remove badly infested and damaged leaves and stems; 2) rinse with water; 3) treat with insecticidal soap or an alcohol solution; 4) place sticky yellow flytraps around the infested plant and others in the vicinity for up to a month to catch remaining whitefly generations.

COMMON DISEASES

Houseplants as a rule live in a clean, controlled environment, at least compared to the outdoors. However, this does not mean that they are immune to conditions that cause disease. Most houseplant diseases are caused by fungus. Since fungus is spread by spores that can survive long periods of time in a dormant state, it is best to keep your houseplant environment free of the spores in the first place. Once your plant has a fungal disease, you can be assured that thousands of spores have already been released into your environment.

The best way to keep this situation under control is to maintain the highest level of plant health. Plants that are vigorous and healthy are less susceptible to diseases and insect infestations. Prevent disease from entering your home by maintaining vigilance, particularly when new plants arrive. Even if you receive a gift from a local florist or high-end shop, you must check the plant thoroughly. If you suspect anything, isolate the plant immediately and monitor it.

Downy Mildew

Downy mildew is found worldwide. It is a fungal disease that thrives in cool and moist conditions. It can spread quickly, so nip this one in the bud, fast.

SYMPTOMS - yellow splotches on the tops of leaves; corresponding white spots on the underside; infection appears on the oldest leaves first; later stages: the yellow spots become large patches and turn gray; the leaf then dies.

PREVENTION - downy mildew likes humidity and coolness; in high humidity, increase the air circulation; monitor plants for early signs of disease; immediately isolate the plant and destroy cuttings that are infected; keep leaves and blooms dry, especially in cool conditions.

ORGANIC CONTROL - 1) cut away all diseased parts of the plant; 2) rinse off the plant; 3) spray with a fungicidal soap; 4) repot in a new, clean pot with fresh, sterile soil; 5) spray with fungicidal soap weekly for a month.

Powdery Mildew

Powdery mildew can affect a wide variety of plants. It thrives in humidity but can also be found in drier conditions because the spores do not need moisture to germinate.

SYMPTOMS - oddly shaped and curled leaves on new growth may precede the infection's white powdery appearance; white or gray floury patches on tops of leaves and flowers; patches turn brown as the disease spreads; leaf and flower death results.

PREVENTION - especially vulnerable plants are kalanchoe and rex begonias; humidity is the main requirement for mildew; increase air circulation by increasing the space between plants.

ORGANIC CONTROL - 1) destroy damaged leaves and stems; 2) wash the leaves and allow them to dry; 3) treat with fungicidal soap; 4) repot in a clean pot with fresh potting mix; 5) treat with fungicidal soap every week for one month.

Sooty Mold

This mold grows on the sweet secretions from insects like aphids, mealybugs, and whiteflies. It generally does not harm the plant if you take care of the infestation before the entire plant is infected.

SYMPTOMS - leaves and stems have a dark gray or black layer of mold; mold can sometimes be wiped off with a cloth; occasionally the surface of the mold will dry out, crack, and separate from the plant; looks like peeling paint; mold does not feed on the plant but does block essential light to the leaves.

PREVENTION - keep leaves free of insects that secrete sweet "honeydew"; wash the sticky substance off the leaves if the plant has been exposed to insects.

ORGANIC CONTROL - 1) wash mold off the leaves with a shower of water; 2) dry leaves; 3) keep insects off plants to prevent reinfection.

Root Rot

This fungus is a killer if left unattended.

SYMPTOMS - newer leaves are smaller than normal; leaves turn yellow and eventually wilt and turn brown; brown or blackened area near the crown (at the soil line); eventually the plant will collapse and die.

PREVENTION - never let the pot become waterlogged; never let plants sit in a pool of water; make sure the soil is composed of a porous potting mix with excellent drainage.

ORGANIC CONTROL - 1) remove the plant from the pot; 2) rinse the roots under the tap until the roots are exposed (handle them gently); 3) lay the plant out on a flat surface and examine the roots; 4) look for brown, mushy roots that are darker than other roots (healthy roots are white and creamy colored); 5) cut off damaged roots with a sharp, clean knife; 6) repot in a new container with new potting soil; you may need to cut away some of the leaves to adjust for the smaller root system. (This procedure is iffy. It is a delicate surgery. Good luck.)

ORGANIC VS. INORGANIC METHODS OF PEST CONTROL

I was raised on a garden philosophy that is largely organically based. Traditionally, country gardeners who live on the lands that their families have lived on for decades, even centuries, study the patterns and seasons and develop a synergistic view of man and land, rather than man versus land. I have inherited that self-sustaining attitude as I was taught early on to work with Mother Nature, not against her. It is called stewardship. It is important that, while being a steward of your land, you remain a steward to *all* land.

Instinctively I look at organic methods to solve my gardening problems or to enhance my garden's assets. I encourage it always, however, this does not mean that I am against all synthetically produced fertilizers and pesticides. I will use them as a last resort but with as much restraint as possible given their proven harm to our soil and environment.

Cost

When it comes to cost, some may say it is too expensive to go organic. But that is no longer the case. Long gone are the days where you have to chase a cow around waiting for it to produce manure to feed your plants. Garden center shelves are full of organic products that you can use. Ask for help when choosing exactly the right product. Now is the time to begin. It is now easier than ever to make the transition.

Why Bother?

What does all of this stewardship have to do with houseplants? A great deal. The small confines our houseplants live in is a microcosm of the greater world. The soil in your planter is still earth. The air in your house is still in constant flow with the air outside. The water and moisture in the room will still return to the atmosphere. It is all related. How we care for any plant in this world does indeed affect the greater good of the earth. Heady stuff? Not really. It is common sense and a sign of respect for all living things who share the resources of this planet.

FREQUENTLY ASKED QUESTIONS

WHERE SHOULD I AVOID PUTTING HOUSEPLANTS?

In the winter (when humidity levels are low), avoid any overhead, table-top, or floor fans. Strong wind will desiccate the plant leaves, making them brittle. Avoid areas exposed to unusually cold or warm temperatures.

My dogs love to sleep in front of the heat/cold registers in our family room – but this is not a suitable home for your houseplants. A basement without windows and/or grow lights is a poor spot for storing or overwintering houseplants. If susceptible to strong winds and the wrong lighting conditions, your home's screened-in-porch is equally bad. Remember, the party is over with the first hint of frost.

No one I know has a greener thumb than my close friend T Lynn Williamson. T Lynn stores his enormous outdoor asparagus ferns, palms, and succulents in a three-car garage. They are kept cozy (above 55 degrees F) all winter with space heaters, waiting until spring to come out to the courtyard for a summer of entertaining.

HOW MUCH DO HOUSEPLANTS COST?

Depending on availability, local competition, size, condition, and species of the plant, the costs of plants may vary considerably. In general, the price of common, smaller plants range from $2.00 to $20.00. Save your change for pots and supplies.

The price of common medium-sized plants range from $10.00 to $70.00. Remember medium houseplants when coming up with better alternatives to expensive yet short-lived cut flowers. Some houseplants live so long they can be passed from generation to generation. My grandmother's white gardenia still thrives in the basement of my family's home. It takes two strong men to move this arrangement outdoors with the changing of seasons.

The larger houseplants can vary in price from $60 to $250 depending on the size of the monster you pick. If your plant is a bit delicate, pay the delivery fee to ensure it gets home safe and sound.

Start your search at the local, price-competitive superstores to pick up the most common plants on your list. You may have to visit your local specialty plant stores or nurseries for the less common varieties. If so, this detour may cost you a bit more at the register.

WHAT SHOULD BE DONE WITH AN UGLY PLANT?

In too many homes, I'll spot one plant that is barely hanging on, kept alive by extraordinary means. Is there not a "code blue" for plants?

It's important to remember that leafless schefflera or struggling succulents are most likely in their poor condition due to disease and pest problems. If the condition persists, it is often best to move them so as not to contaminate healthy plants.

Unless you have a strong sentimental attachment to a particular plant, it might be best to retire them. Yes, trash them. Minimize your pain and suffering by replacing the sentimental plant from Aunt Judy with a far healthier plant of the same species. If Aunt Judy might object, you don't have to tell her.

CAN HOUSEPLANTS BE TAKEN OUTDOORS?

With some precautions, I think it is beneficial to take your plants (especially those with large, waxy leaves) for an occasional break outdoors. Acid rain is actually beneficial in cleansing plants of accumulated dust and insects, and many diseases. I often use common tropical plants (elephant ears, corn plant, etc.) in my exterior designs. Check with your local garden expert or agricultural agent regarding the expected first frost. Repot your tropical plants for overwintering indoors well before "D" (first frost) Day.

CAN DIFFERENT HOUSEPLANTS BE COMBINED IN THE SAME POT?

I believe the secrets to my success as an exterior garden designer are my combinations of plantings. I remain unafraid to experiment, and am more than happy to do a little plant rearranging given occasional poor results. If only there was an online dating service for plants. . .

Most often I use a smaller plant specimen as an underplanting of a larger plant, especially if the "legs" (stalks) on the larger plant aren't so attractive. If the marriage is to work, each plant must enjoy the same water and light conditions. So if you're wondering if the cactus/fern combination is out – the answer is yes (sorry).

To produce the most attractive arrangements, combine plants with distinctively different leaves. Try underplanting a fiddle leaf fig with the small leaf ivy or a Chinese fan palm atop a rabbits foot fern.

HOW IMPORTANT IS SOIL?

Your key to plant success is the soil you use. Do not assume that every brand of soil sold at your local plant depot is quality soil. Poorer brands contain filler such as rock, concrete, hays, and grasses. If I'm not willing to play in the soil with my bare hands because I detect contaminants, dull tan color or a dry, dusty appearance, it's not coming home with me. Like Miracle-Gro®, the soil you select should be a rich brown in color and smooth to the touch, sifting easily through your hands.

WHAT TOOLS WILL I NEED?

A spade, watering cans (needle nose and large spout), a water sprayer, hand clippers, and your own pair of miniature scissors – this collection is all you will need for most interior gardening.

Remember one thing when borrowing your mom's pair of scissors: "When Momma ain't happy, nobody's happy!" It's best to get your own pair.

SHOULD ARTIFICIAL PLANTS EVER BE USED?

Would you serve a plastic turkey at Thanksgiving? Treat yourself and others to living, breathing plants.

DO INDOOR PLANTS MAKE A GOOD GIFT?

Will the birthday boy or girl miss the bottle of wine or liquor you surprised him or her with last year? Not likely given the dozens of wrapped wine bottles already huddled on the foyer table. With some research, the right plant could make the perfect gift. Plants make perfect host/hostess gifts, house warming presents, get well gifts, etc. First, consider the best growing conditions for the plant, the likelihood the recipients will care for the plant, their interior design preference, and their time-away schedule.

Provide your friend with a note regarding plant care and plant points of interest. To relieve any gift anxiety, reassure your friend that your relationship will remain solid despite the plant's future. Plants are to be enjoyed. Should misfortune strike, they can always be replaced.

HOW MANY PLANTS SHOULD I HAVE IN A ROOM?

When adding plants to any room, I recommend restraint. In most homes, the secret to creating a beautiful room is removing the clutter. Most of us could afford to remove 50 percent of the stuff we already have. Therefore, I think it's best not to make the same mistake when adding plants.

In any room, begin your introduction to plants with one or two plants. Add others over time according to your taste. Be careful; too many plants may create the appearance of a funeral parlor.

On a piece of furniture or a countertop, I usually prefer the look of a single, "perfect" plant over a collection. Should you like a collection of plants, I prefer repetition of the same color or style of plant.

MEET JON CARLOFTIS

Jon Carloftis, the youngest of six children, grew up on the banks of the Rockcastle River in the foothills of the Appalachian Mountains. There he began a love affair with nature that led to recognition as one of the nation's premier garden designers. He attended the University of Kentucky where he earned a degree in communications and also studied horticulture. In 1988 he moved to New York

City, introducing himself to the Upper East Side as a rooftop garden designer, via a few kind doormen and simple business cards. Delighted clients soon passed his name along to fellow art collectors, entrepreneurs, and entertainers, all eager for fresh, innovative garden designs.

Jon has designed gardens for such celebrities as Jerry and Linda Bruckheimer, Julianne Moore and Edward Norton. His renowned designs have graced the pages of *Country Gardens, Country Home, Garden Design, House Beautiful, Martha Stewart Living,* and *Metropolitan Home.* He has been featured on HGTV, the *Martha Stewart Living* television show, and the Style channel. Jon is the garden expert for HGTV's Trend Smart Advisory Board. Jon is the recipient of a landscape design award from the Museum of the City of New York, and is the author of the book *First a Garden.*

As a lecturer, Jon continues to charm audiences with good humor, elegant manners, and an unpretentious approach to making the world a little greener, and a little more beautiful.

To learn more about Jon Carloftis, visit www.joncarloftis.com. For information about Jon's garden lecture series, visit www.mckinneyspeakers.com.